KORUMA
eros!
ZIHNI

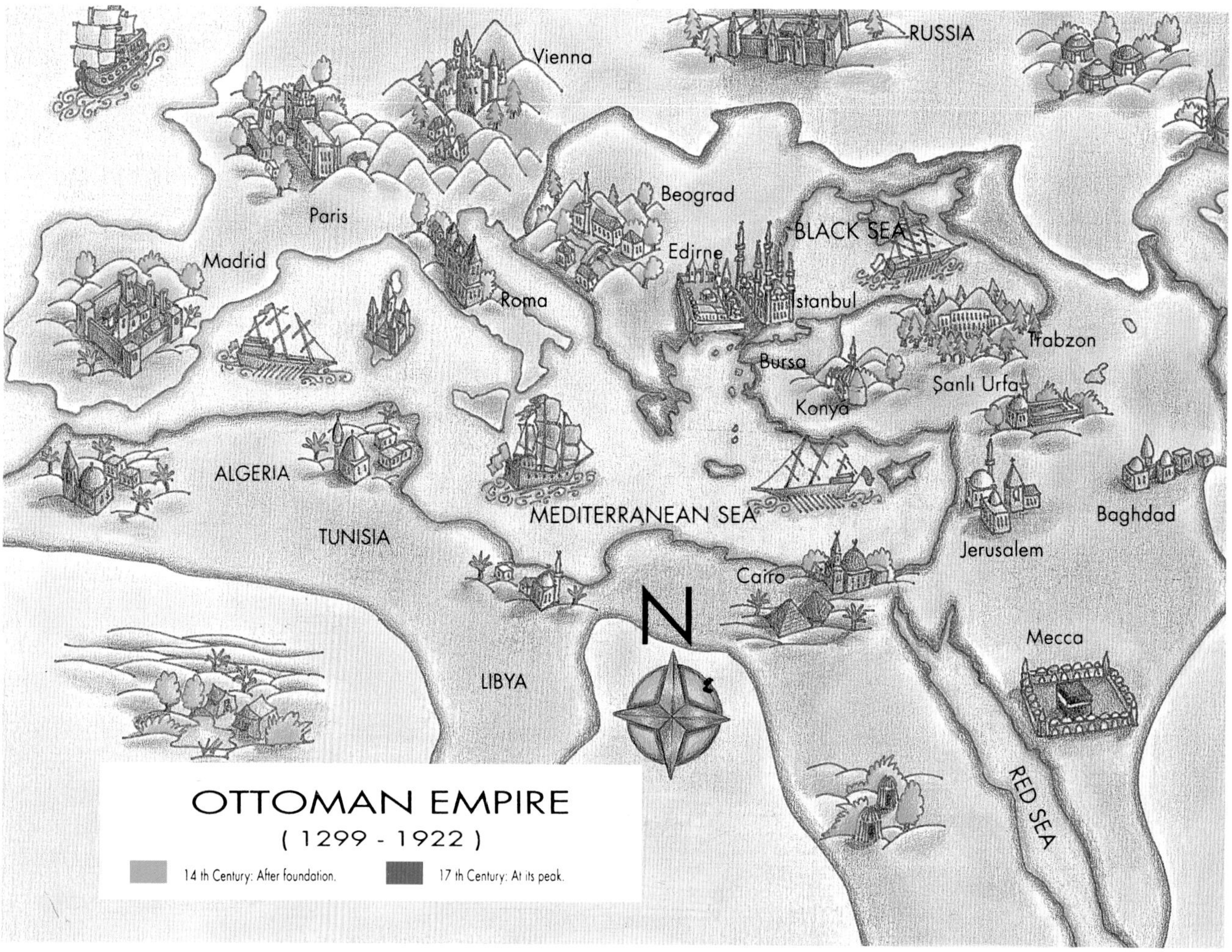

THE OTTOMAN EMPIRE (1299-1922)

Central Asia was the homeland of the Turks. Over the centuries, they either migrated in large groups or organized military expeditions to various regions in Asia and even to Central Europe. Early in the 7th century, these nomadic Turkish tribes started to settle and establish states. The most important one was the small Ottoman Principality in Asia Minor which grew into the powerful Ottoman Empire that lasted for six hundred years. Although the Ottomans constituted the minority in the lands they conquered, due to their superior ability to organize and administrate efficiently, they governed these lands and secured a peaceful life for their subjects (Jews, Christians and Moslems) regardless of race, religion, culture or nationality. For almost four hundred years, the Ottoman Empire ruled the lands extending from the Arabian peninsula to Russia, from Persia to the Balkans, Greece and as far as Vienna. Towards the end of the 19th century, the different nations under Ottoman rule, agitated by foreign powers, started to revolt, thereby weakening the internal structure of the empire. World War I was the final blow that brought on the collapse of the Ottoman Empire along with its allies. The lands of the empire were divided among the victors, but Kemal Atatürk led the Turkish nation to victory after a war for independence, and established the foundation of the Republic of Turkey on the remains of the Ottoman Empire, in 1923.

THE TOPKAPI PALACE

SABAHATTİN TÜRKOĞLU

NET®
TURİSTİK YAYINLAR
SANAYİ VE TİCARET A.Ş.

CONTENTS

Published and distributed by:

NET TURİSTİK YAYINLAR A.Ş.

Şifa Hamamı Sok. No. 18/2, 34400 Sultanahmet-İstanbul/Turkey
Tel: (90-212) 516 32 28 - 516 82 61 Fax: (90-212) 516 84 68

236. Sokak No.96/B Funda Apt., 35360 Hatay/İzmir/Turkey
Tel:(90-232) 228 78 51-250 69 22 Fax: (90-232) 250 22 73

Kışla Mah., 54. Sok., İlteray Apt., No.11/A-B, 07040 Antalya/Turkey
Tel: (90-242) 248 93 67 - 243 14 97 Fax: (90-242) 248 93 68

Eski Kayseri Cad., Dirikoçlar Apt. No.45, 50200 Nevşehir/Turkey
Tel: (90-384) 213 30 89 - 213 46 20 Fax: (90-384) 213 40 36

Text: **Sabahattin Türkoğlu**
Translation: **Nüket Eraslan**
Photographs: **Tahsin Aydoğmuş, İrfan Ertel, Nadir Ede, Haluk Özözlü**
Layout: **Not Ajans**
Typesetting: **AS & 64 Ltd. Şti.**
Colour Separation: **Çali Grafik A.Ş.**
Printed in Turkey by: **Asır Matbaacılık Ltd. Şti.**

ISBN 975-479-234-8

1st Edition, 1995

The historical peninsula on which the Topkapı Palace is located (as seen from Galata, 19th. century).

ESTABLISHMENT, LOCATION, ENVIRONS

The area occupied by the Topkapı Palace extends from Sarayburnu to the Church of Haghia Sophia. It is surrounded by a high wall called **Sur-i-Sultani** (Imperial Wall) which is fortified with towers, and has seven gates. Four of these gates are on the side facing the sea. The most important gate is Babı-ı-Hümayun (Imperial Gate), located behind Haghia Sophia. It took approximately thirteen years (1465-1478) to complete the construction of the palace, including the wall.

New additions constructed during the reign of each succeeding sultan changed and enlarged the original plan of the palace. The inscriptions pertaining to the construction, and the tughras (Imperial signatures) found on the walls of the buildings indicate the reign during which these changes, additions and renovations took place.

The Old Palace, the New Palace

After conquering Istanbul, Fatih Sultan Mehmet (the Conqueror) built a palace for himself in Beyazıt, where the university is located today. He lived there for a while and later moved into the palace he had built at Sarayburnu. During his reign, the palace at Beyazıt was called the Old Palace and the one at Sarayburnu, the New Palace.

Originally, a summer palace located by the sea at the tip of Sarayburnu was called Topkapı. After it burned in 1862, the New Palace, in its entirety, came to be known as the Topkapı Palace.

Relocation from the Old palace to the New Palace took place in stages. First, the government and military offices, then the Harem were moved.

It is said that Hürrem Sultan (Roxelane), one of the wives of Sultan Süleyman (Süleyman the Magnificent), was the first woman to move into the new Harem. Once the Sultan's harem moved completely into the new palace (Topkapı Palace), the old palace became the residence of the wives and concubines of the dead sultans.

The Ottoman documents state that Fatih Sultan Mehmet could not find a habitable building belonging to the Byzantine era. However, as scholars indicated and recent discoveries have proven, there are remains of old structures both on the hill and at the bottom of the hill. The basement of the building

Top: Topkapı Palace as seen from the sea. *The Imperial Gate.*

An aerial view of the Topkapı Palace.

which today houses the Treasury, the Gots column (St. Simeon, 5th century) which stands on the Saraybumu side and the remains of old structures discovered during excavations carried on both inside the Palace and the Sea of Marmara side prove this. Historians mention the existence of three Greek temples in this area during the time of Theodosius. The one built for the Sun God was converted into a big church (probably Haghia Sophia). The other two were also converted into churches. The Church of Haghia Irene, located in the first courtyard, was probably one of them. Undoubtedly, old temples were torn down and new churches, using some of the original materials of the temples, were built at the same site.

The origin of the capital and parts of the colossal column located in front of the kitchens seen after one passes through the second gate, Bâbü's-Selam (Gate of Peace), is not known. They belong to the 5th and 6th centuries.

The strategic location of the hill, the aesthetic beauty of the area called the Olive Grove and the view it commands are probably the reasons Fatih Sultan Mehmet chose this site to build a new palace. The palace grounds cover an area of approximately 600,000 square meters, and today, the main buildings are used as a museum. During the Empire, large private gardens of the sultan, vegetable gardens, game fields and pavilions and kiosks covered the rest of the area. Today, Çinili Köşk (Tiled Pavilion) and Sepetçiler Pavilion still stand, and the Has Bahçe (private gardens of the sultans) has been turned into a public park (Gülhane Parkı).

The palace consists of courtyards connected to each other with large gates, and the Harem. In the West, it was important to build the gates of a palace on the same axis, and monuments were placed on these axes. At Topkapı, however, the gates are neither located on an axis nor are there any monuments. Actually, at Topkapı, simplicity and modesty prevail.

The four consecutive courtyards cover an area approximately 370 meters long and 220 meters wide. Bab-ı Hümayun is followed by the first courtyard. Bâbü's-Selam, or the Mid-Gate, is followed by the second courtyard, and Bâbü'ssa'âde or the Akağalar Gate (Gate of the White Eunuchs) leads into the third courtyard. The fourth courtyard, which

Plan of the Topkapı Palace

1- The 1st. courtyard.
2- The Babü's selam Gate.
3- The 2nd. courtyard.
4- Entrance to the Harem.
5- The Kubbealtı and the Tower of Justice.
6- The Weapons Section.
7- The Akağalar Gate.
8- The European Porcelains Section.
9- The Kitchens (the Chinese and Japanese Porcelains Section).
10- The Turkish Porcelains Section.
11- The Arz Odası.
12- The 3rd. courtyard.
13- The Sultans' Costumes Section.
14- The Treasury Section.
15- The Library of Ahmet III.
16- The Offices of the Museum.
17- The Inscriptions, Miniatures and Sultans' Portraits Section.
18- The Clocks Section.
19- The Sacred Relics Section.
20- The Library of the Topkapı Palace.
21- The Sofa Mosque.
22- The Mecidiye Pavilion.
23- The Head Physician's Room.
24- The Mustafa Paşa Pavilion.
25- The 4th. courtyard.
26- The Revan Pavilion.
27- The Baghdad Pavilion.
28- The Circumcision Room.
29- The Pavilion of Abdülhamit I.
30- The Courtyard of the Favorites.
31- The Room of Sultan Murat III.
32- The Hünkar Sofası.
33- The Courtyard of the Valide Sultan.
34- The Hospital in the Harem.
35- The Courtyard of the Karaağalar.
36- The Privy Stables.
37- The Bookstore.

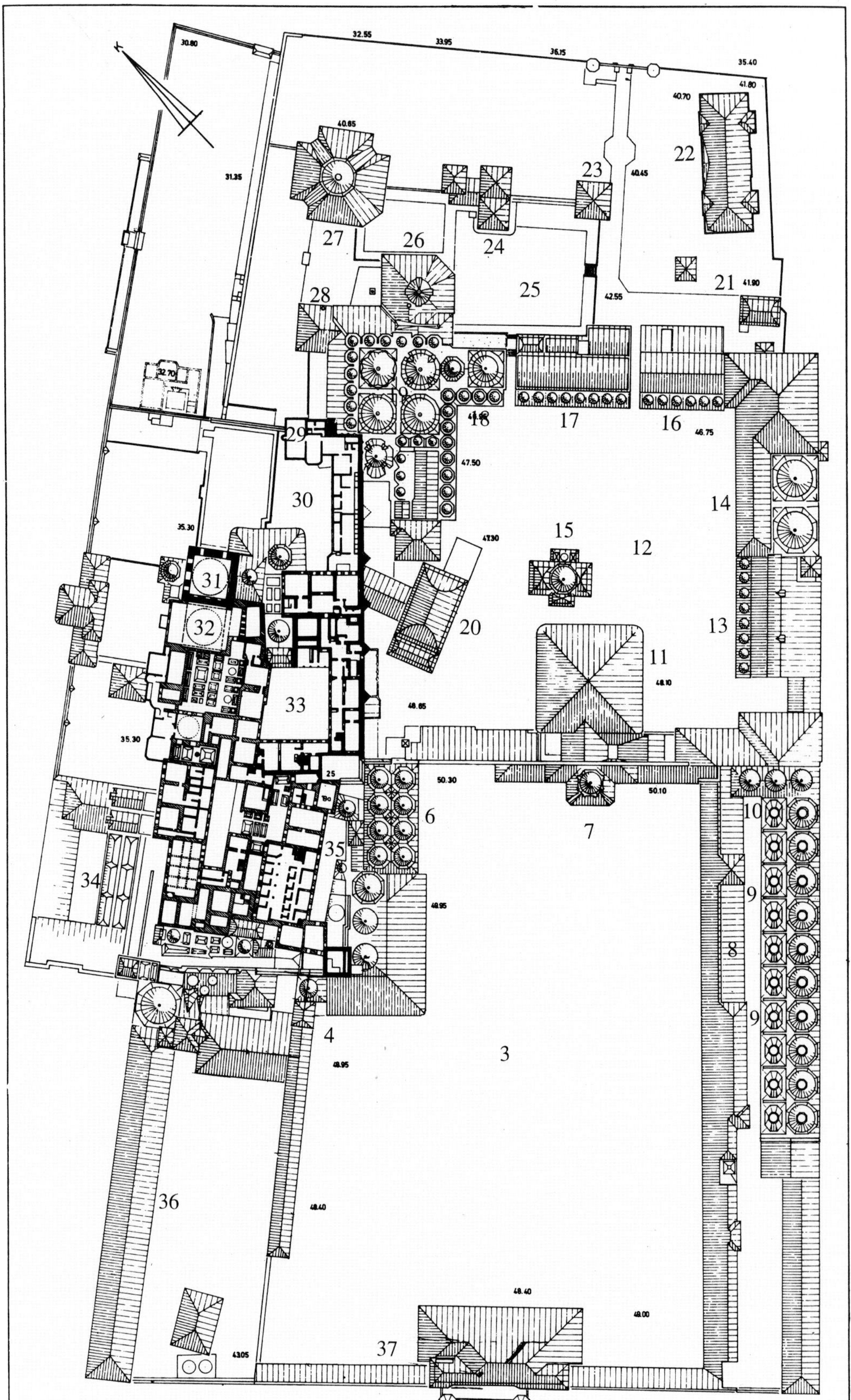

The Topkapı Palace as seen from the air.

follows, is also called **Lala Bahçesi** (the garden of the male servants in charge of Sultan's children).

The palace buildings lack unity and uniformity due to many reasons. Each sultan, according to his own taste and needs, ordered the construction of new buildings. The architects who built them had different points of view, used different styles, and their personality, quality of work and education differed.

The changes and additions made to accommodate the pressing needs turned the palace, especially the Harem, into a disorganized complex. Many changes were made after natural disasters, such as fires and earthquakes. Therefore, rather than a palace, Topkapı today should be viewed as a museum of architecture, where different phases of Turkish architecture over the centuries are displayed, The major constructions which took place are as follows:

- Construction of the palace began during the reign of Fatih Sultan Mehmet (1478).
- After the earthquake, which historians refer to as the "lesser doomsday," extensive restorations took place during the reign of Beyazıt II (1512).
- After his campaign to Egypt, Yavuz Sultan Selim built the Privy Room to store the sacred relics he had brought, and the section of the Harem attached to this room (1512-1520).
- During the reign of Murat III, the kitchens, which had been ruined by a fire, some sections of the Harem and the quarters of the Zülüflü Baltacılar (Halberdiers) were restored (1574-1595).
- After the fire in the Harem, extensive reconstruction was carried on during the reign of Mehmet IV (1648-1687).
- Major additions and restorations, especially in the Harem, took place during the reigns of Mahmut I, Osman III, Abdülhamit II, Selim III and Mahmut II. The inscription plates with tughras indicate that during the reign of Mahmut II many buildings were restored.

The tughras and the dates on the inscription plates found on the gates and the walls at various locations in the palace do not necessarily indicate that the particular structure was built or repaired by the named sultan. The inscriptions were changed due to various reasons, or replaced by inscriptions which praised the reigning sultan. In addition, the custom of placing the tughra on the inscription plate was begun after Mahmut II.

The Topkapı Palace, 2nd. courtyard (a miniature from the 16th century Hünername).

Soğukçeşme Street and Haghia Eirene (in the front), the Topkapı Palace (in the background).

BAB-I HUMAYUN (THE IMPERIAL GATE) AND THE FIRST COURTYARD

Bab-ı-Hümayun is the main entrance through the wall surrounding the palace grounds. Located behind Haghia Sophia, it is the largest and the most important gate of the palace. It was built during the reign of Fatih Sultan Mehmet and restored by Mahmut II and Sultan Abdülaziz. Their tughras are seen on the gate. Entrances and exits through this gate were accompanied by ceremonies.

Inside, there are rooms on each side for the gate keepers. As we can tell from the old records and miniatures, Fatih Sultan Mehmet had a pavilion built on this gate. It was called the Alay (Procession) Pavilion, but later it collapsed.

The first courtyard is entered via the Imperial Gate. Some of the old service buildings of the palace, such as the administrations of the imperial estates, the hospital, the wood depot, the lion houses, the gunpowder depot and the private bakery, located on both sides of the courtyard, do not exist anymore. However, Haghia Irene and Darphane (the mint), located to the left, which were once used as armories, are in good condition. Today, Haghia Irene, built in the 6th century, is a museum. The jewelry, and the gold and silver utensils of the palace were also made in the mint. Deavi Pavilion, one of the most interesting buildings, which does not exist today, was a small building located on the right, in front of the Mid-Gate. Every day, one of the viziers accepted petitions from the public and took them to the Divan (Council of State) to be discussed. Apparently, the first courtyard was open to anyone who had a compaint or wish. The Admonition Plate and Siyaset Çeşmesi (Fountain of Politics), which was the site of executions, were next to the wall on the right.

The other entrance into the first courtyard is the Gülhane Park Gate, which used to be called the Soğukçeşme Gate. The sultans used to watch the parades from **Alay Pavilion,** built in 1806 on the wall surrounding the palace grounds. It faces Bab-ı-Âli, which was the office of the Grand Vizier.

The wall that stretches along the Sea of Marmara side of the first courtyard was built in this century. The buildings housing the various services of the palace were located behind it.

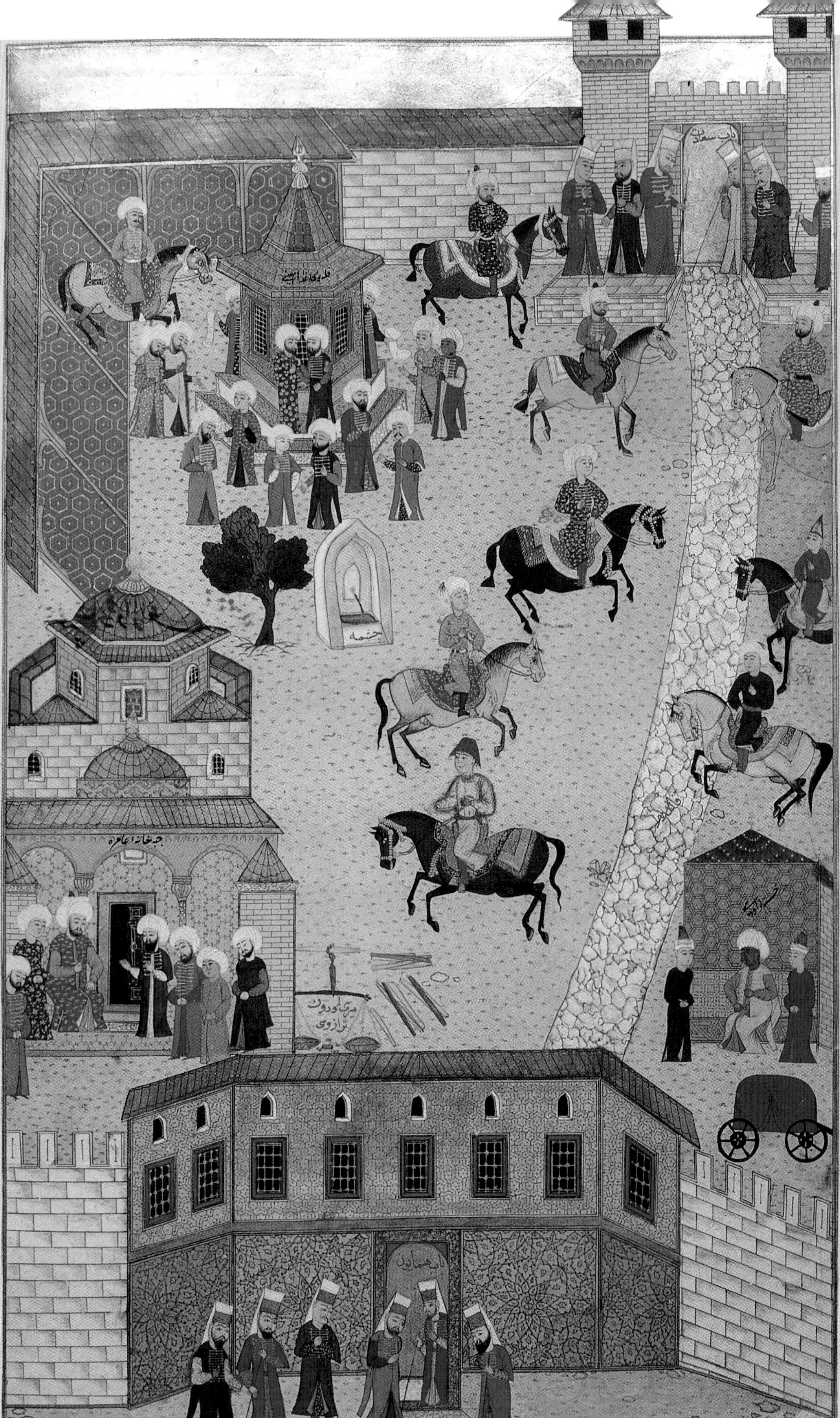

Topkapı Palace, 1st. courtyard (16th century).

Interior view of the 2nd gate (Babü's-selam).

Exterior view of the 2nd. Gate (Babü's-selam).

BABÜ'S-SELÂM (The Mid-Gate) AND THE SECOND COURTYARD

Today, **the Mid-Gate is the entrance to the museum. With its conical capped towers** located on each side and its battlements, this gate resembles medieval castles. It is said that after Kanuni Sultan Süleyman's Eastern Europe campaign, the towers were built under the influence of the castles seen during the campaign. Yet, sources indicate the existence of the two towers in the 15th century. The date 1524 is inscribed on its iron door.

Inside the gate, there are rooms for the gate keepers on both sides. In the history of the Topkapı Palace, this area was called **Kapı Arası** (gate courtyard), where viziers and other state leaders were detained just before leaving the gate. Actually, there are dark rooms, resembling dungeons, in the towers. The Grand Viziers used to come on horseback to this gate and then walk in. Although the outside of the gate has a military look, the side facing the second courtyard is quite charming. There is a wide portico with a decorated ceiling and eaves. The decoration of the eaves are predominately 18th century Baroque. The facade of the gate is decorated with religious inscriptions and tughras of different sultans. The second courtyard was also called Alay Meydanı (Procession Square). Some of the most important events in the history of the palace and Ottoman Empire took place here. Kubbealtı, the building from where the Ottoman Empire was ruled for four hundred years, is located in this courtyard. The janissaries were paid their salaries (ulufe) and feasts in their honor were held here. Receptions of foreign ambassadors, Ayak Divan (a council held in haste in the sultan's presence), which took place in front of the Akağalar Gate, holiday greetings and other ceremonies, such as paying homage, took place in this courtyard.

There are very important and rare finds and structures belonging to the Byzantine era. Various canals and a cistern have been found under the wide road that goes through the center of the courtyard. The brick covering of the cistern is still visible. As mentioned before, excavations carried on along the west side of the courtyard unearthed colossal column capitals belonging to the 5th and 6th centuries and sarcophagi made of porphyry. Two of the sar-

cophagi unearthed are seen in the courtyard of Haghia Irene. During Byzantine era, sarcophagi made of porphyry were used for the emperors and members of the royal family. Therefore, it may be assumed that buildings like churches and mausoluems existed here at that time. It is not probable that these sarcophagi were brought here from other parts of Istanbul upon the orders of sultans. If that were the case then they would not have been left underground. The courtyard is surrounded by a **colonnade**. Behind the colonnade, on the right, are the **buildings which housed the kitchens** and on the left are the **Quarters of the Helberdiers** and **Privy Stables. The exit** (today the entrance) **of the Harem,** the Kubbealtı, where the Grand Vizier and viziers met, and, next to it, the old treasury, which is today houses the Weapons Section as the Museum of Arms, are located on the north corner of the courtyard. A wide road connects the Mid-Gate and the **Akağalar** Gate, which are not on the same axis. The Akağalar Gate (White Eunuch's Gate), which is also called the Bab-üs-Saade (the Gate of Felicity) also attracts the attention.

The Babü's-selam Gate (the 2nd. Gate).

Exterior view of the Weapons Section.

The Kitchens as seen from the 2nd. courtyard.

The Courtyard of the Kitchens.

THE KITCHENS

From the second courtyard, there ara three entrances into the area where the kitchens are located. These entrances, in order, are: Kileri Amire, Has Mutfak, and Helvahane kapısı. The buildings which once housed the kitchens are arranged in a row along both sides of a long street paved with stone. The view is quite picturesque. The two buildings across from the first entrance called the Kileri Amire (The Main Pantry) were the old pantry and the creamery. Today fabrics and **archives** are stored here. The buildings facing these used to be the quarters of the caretakers. It has been renovated and today it is a repair shop used for the maintainance of the museum. As one advances north, the wooden house seen on the Sea of Marmara side is the old **Aşçılar (cooks) Mosque** and the quarters of the cooks used to be across from it. One of these buildings today houses the Silverware and European Porcelains section. Adjacent to the **Aşçılar Mosque** are the palace kitchens where today the Chinese and Japanese porcelains are displayed. After the fire in

The Courtyard of the Kitchens.

The Kitchens, a view of the Helvahane.

1574, the architect (Mimar) Sinan rebuilt these kitchens and enlarged them. The **cylindrical chimneys** are characteristic of that period. A small mosque and **Helvahane** where confectionary was prepared were located at the end of the street and today, Istanbul Glassware and Porcelains are displayed here.

Every day, meals for approximately four thousand people were prepared in these kitchens. Different meals were served to the members of the Harem and the palace employees.

METAL KITCHEN UTENSILS SECTION

Among the buildings which housed the kitchens, the building where the metal kitchen utensils are displayed is the most interesting, since the giant kettles used to prepare meals for the members of the palace, service sets and other tools are found here. The rest of these buildings have been turned into exhibit halls, and thus have lost their identity. Cooking pans, copper dishes, bowls, round metal trays, cop-

A cook carrying a plate of confectionary.

The Kitchens.

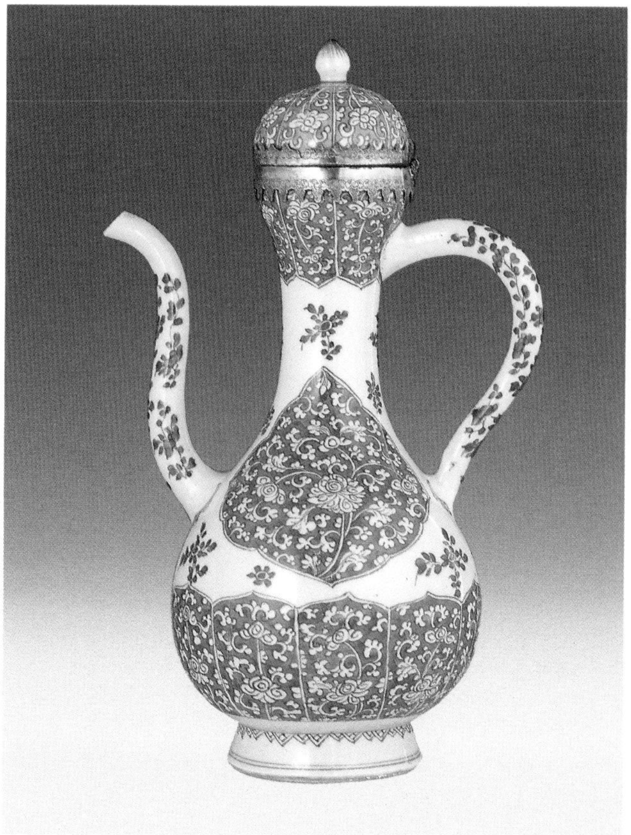

The Annam Vase (15th century) and a blue-white pitcher (Ming Dynasty).

A blue-white vase converted into a rosewater dispenser.

per jugs with handles and coffee grinders are embellished with typical Turkish motifs. Some of them have inscriptions indicating the date they were made, the storeroom in which they belonged and the name of the donor. Most of these were made from wrought copper embellished by scraping and chiseling techniques.

After the 18th century, tombak (mercury plated copper) vessels became popular. There are a few Seljuk objects and most of them are mortars.

There are only a few candlesticks made in the 15th and 16th centuries and the rest of the objects belong to the 17th, 18th and 19th centuries.

THE CHINESE PORCELAINS SECTION

In the early years of the Ottoman Empire, traditional copper and baked-clay pots were used to serve food in the palace. Gold and silver pots and plates became popular later, during the prosperous period of the empire.

Two Celadon pitchers.

A cobalt blue pitcher.

Toward the middle of the 16th century, the use of imported Chinese porcelainware became a tradition in the palace because Chinese porcelains were durable, elegant, of high quatily, and they were expensive imported ware which could be afforded only by rich people and the palaces of prosperous countries of the world, like the Ottoman Empire. There was also a rumor that **Celadon Porcelainware** could expose poisoned food!

The number of Chinese porcelainware in the palace is over ten thousand. Due to the number and variety of these Chinese porcelains in the Topkapı Palace, this collection is among the few in the world.

Even though Chinese pottery dates back to 1500 B.C., it started gaining fame during the 5th dynasty and later became a major export product. The Middle Eastern countries were the first to import these porcelains in the 10th century. As a matter of fact, the oldest Chinese porcelainware found in the palace was made in the 10th century. These first came to the palace, not from China, but from other Middle Eastern countries where Chinese porcelains were imported. Records indicate that Yavuz Sultan Selim,

after seeing the high quatiy of these porcelains during his campaign to Egypt and Iran, brought them to the Topkapı Palace and most of the succeeding sultans continued to import them. European countries discovered these porcelains much later.

The Chinese porcelainware at the palace can be divided into four groups according to the Chinese dynasties:

The Song Dynasty (960-1279) porcelains.
The Yuan Dynasty (1280-1368) porcelains.
The Ming Dynasty (1368-1644) porcelains.
The Ch'ing Dynasty (1644-1912) porcelains.
and also according to the technique used:

- Celadons
- Blue and white porcelains
- Monochrome porcelains
- Polychrome porcelains

Products of the **Song Dynasty** were unsurpassed in quality, quantity and variety.

Since Celadons were shipped from the port of Martaban in Burma, they are called **Martabani** by the Turks. There is an impressive number of them in the palace. They are famous for their pale green col-

A multi colored pitcher (Ming Dynasty).

A Celadon plate.

A Celadon plate.

or, hard glaze and thickness. Celadons were decorated usually with dragon and fish motifs, but plant motifs and geometric designs in relief were also used. There are celadon plates, pitchers, vases and cups. Cobalt, which is used to color porcelain blue, was known in Islamic lands, especially in Iran, back in the 11th century. After importing cobalt, the Chinese achieved great advances in porcelain production and as a result the blue and white porcelains were produced. The method of using cobalt under glaze started in China during the 14th century and continued until the 19th century. The most beautiful ware made in cobalt blue belong to the Yuan and Ming dynasties.

Most of the blue and white porcelains of the collection belong to the Ming dynasty. The Annam (Vietnam) vase, with its cylindrical neck and wide belly is quite interesting, since it is dated 1450.

During the **Ming Dynasty,** porcelainware was exported in large quantities to European countries, too. In the collection, there are many large Kraak plates decorated with cartouche designs, plates with rough decorations, small jars with handles, brown or

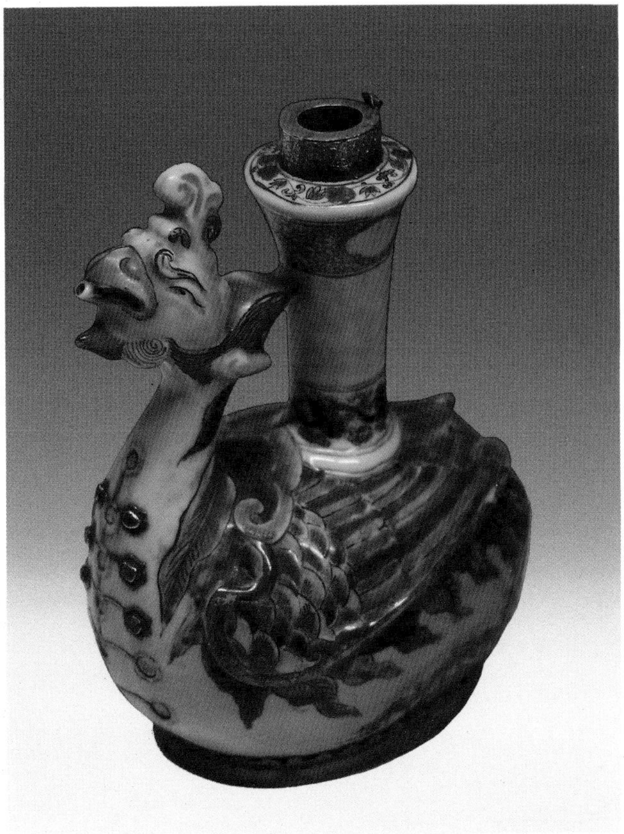

A dragon-shaped pitcher.

A blue-white plate (14th century).

A blue-white plate (14th century).

Japanese vases.

A Japanese vase (19th century).

navy blue glazed cups, plates and pitchers which are typical examples of Ming Dynasty porcelains. The white bowls decorated with multicolored lines, and the plain yellow bowls were made during this period, also.

The porcelainware exported in large quantities to the western countries in the 16th century was usually made according to the tastes and specifications of each country. There are some made especially for the Topkapı Palace. On these there are inscriptions written in Arabic and verses from the Koran. Some of these were especially ordered by the Chinese emperors to be presented to the reigning sultan. While viewing the collection certain pitchers, cups and jars studded with jewels and with curved handles and caps attract attention. These embellishment were added to these pieces by the palace craftsmen.

The production which had stopped briefly during the Ch'ing dynasty resumed after personal efforts of emperor K'ang-hsi and exports increased again. During this period, production of the blues and whites continued, and two new varities called the **"pink family"** and **"green family,"** due to their color, were introduced.

JAPANESE PORCELAINS SECTION

The Japanese Porcelains found at the Topkapı Palace Museum were made in Japan for export in the 17th and 18th centuries. Since they were shipped from the port of Imari, they are called "Imari Porcelains." There are seven hundred and thirty of these in the museum and they were used for decorative purposes.

ISTANBUL GLASSWARE AND PORCELAINS SECTION

Serious production of glass and porcelainware in Turkey began in the 19th century as a result of the personal interest and efforts of the sultans.

Among the objects displayed, those made of glass and Lüleci clay are traditional Turkish crafts. The cigarette holders, mouth pieces for water pipes, coffee cups and saucers, writing sets, etc., made from brown, blue or natural colored Lüleci clay are called **Tophane Crafts** and they are gilded.

Most of the Çeşmibülbüls (a kind of precious

A bowl with a lid (A Yıldız Porcelainware).

A view of the Porcelains Section.

Turkish made glassware decorated with spiral lines), opals, colored glassware, cut glass and crystalware were produced in the workshops located on the Anatolian side of Istanbul. These are known as **Beykoz Crafts** and all of them were produced in the 19th century. The first porcelain factory was established in Beykoz during the reign of Sultan Abdülmecit. The porcelains produced here had the same high quality as the porcelains produced in Vienna and Saxony. They were stamped **Eser-i-Istanbul** and carried the **sign of the star and crescent.** The factory produced mainly for the palace. The gifts the sultans presented were made here, too.

After this factory closed down, a new factory was founded on the grounds of the **Yıldız Palace** by Abdülhamit II. **The Yıldız Porcelain Factory,** where both Turkish and foreign designers and craftsmen worked, also produced mainly for the palace. The vases, plates and tea sets produced here are decorated by **Roman** motifs, flowers and landscapes. Some of the tea sets are decorated with the portraits of all the sultans and some carry the tughra of Abdülhamit II. Everything produced here was signed and dated.

EUROPEAN PORCELAINS SECTION

This is one of the richest collections (five thousand pieces) in the Topkapı Palace Museum. The porcelain factory in Turkey was founded at a time when the palace became interested in European porcelains. Abdülhamit II was personally involved in the establishment of the factory. Even a small museum housing the European porcelains was established at the Yıldız Palace during his reign. Close political relations with France influenced this project. Most of the European porcelains were moved to the Topkapı Palace from the Yıldız Palace. Almost all of these were gifts from European countries. The collection consists of German, Viennese and Russian porcelains. They were made in the 18th and 19th centuries.

There are many pieces belonging to the different periods of the **Meissen factory of Germany** and the **Berlin Porcelain Factory.** The **Viennese porcelains,** which were made from hard clay, have Chinese style motifs on red background.

French porcelains, like **Sevre, Limoges,** and

Fountainbleau occupy an important place in the collection.

Examples of Czechoslovakian **(Bohemian) crystals,** which were the most famous in Europe, as well as **Venetian, Irish, French** crystals and various other glassware are displayed here. These were all given as gifts to the palace.

The technique used in the production and the design of these crystals are typically European. Since they were gifts, very few Turkish motifs or shapes were used.

SILVERWARE SECTION

Only a small portion of the three-thousand pieces that make up the collection is on display. Silver objects were used extensively in the Ottoman palace. They were made either in the workshops of the palace or at various other workshops in Istanbul, and presented to the sultans as gifts. Some were gifts from foreign countries.

The oldest silver object in the collection is a silver bowl which belonged to Kanuni Sultan

Yıldız porcelains (19th century).

A Swedish vase (19th century).

The silver motif on the Fountain of Ahmet III.

Süleyman and his tughra is inscribed on the bowl. There are numerous other silver objects in various shapes bearing the tughras of sultans İbrahim, Mehmet IV, Ahmet III, Abdülaziz and Abdülhamit IV. Also, there are many silver objects ordered by the princessess. As a matter of fact, even the European silver objects, which have different shapes and ornamentations, are stamped.

The gifts presented to Abdülhamit II on the 25th anniversary of his reign occupy an important place in this collection. Models of buildings, monuments, fountains, etc. made of silver are among these gifts. Examples of French, English and Russian-made silver objects are also displayed in this section.

WEAPONS SECTION

The weapons displayed in the building which housed the old treasury are a small portion of a very extensive collection of the Topkapı Palace.

The main sources of this rich collection are the valuable weapons left behind by the enemy, the weapons made in various workshops in the Empire, especially the ones made in the workshops of the palace, and the gifts sent to the palace by foreign rulers.

According to the tradition, the sultans and **Turkish leaders** used to store their weapons in the palace. But the oldest weapons came to the palace after Yavuz Sultan Selim's Egypt campaign. These are very valuable and important from the point of view of the history of the art of weapon-making. Yavuz Sultan Selim brought to the palace the weapons of the kings and commanders he fought, and the **swords of the Islamic leaders,** particularly those of the Prophet Mohammed and the four khalifs, which are invaluable to the Islamic world. Since then, in addition to Turkish arms, many **Arab, Mameluke** and **Persian** arms accumulated in the treasury of the palace.

Persian, Mameluke and Turkish swords have certain characteristics in common. Originally, they were made straight with two blades. Later, their shapes varied and finally they were made curved with a single blade. Fatih Sultan Mehmet's sword is a good example of a Turkish sword.

The armor has certain common characteristics, too. It is made of mail and reinforced by steel plates to cover the sensitive parts of the body.

Shirts, with names of the religious leaders and

Top: An armor for a horse head (16th century).

An Ottoman helmet.

verses from the Koran written on them, were worn under the armor. These names and verses were inscribed on the metal plates of the armor, too. In this section, different shaped helmets, axes, hatchets, bows and arrows, and spears belonging to Persians, Mamelukes and Turks are displayed. Even though few in number, European arms, which were either presented to the palace or seized in wars, as well as an Indian shield and a Japanese armor are included in the collection.

Among the firearms, there are many rifles and guns embellished with ivory and mother-of-pearl inlay and precious metals and jewels. They belong to the 17th, 18th and 19 th centuries.

Very valuable jewelled weapons have been moved to the Treasury Section after the Topkapı Palace became a museum. Weapons of the Prophet Mohammed and religious leaders are displayed at the Sacred Relics Section.

An Ottoman armour and helmet (15th century).

A shield with flower designs (16th century).

The Tower of Justice.

The Tower of Justice as seen from the 3rd. courtyard.

KUBBEALTI (THE COURT OF THE VIZIERS COUNCIL)

Viziers and other state leaders conducted the affairs of the state and passed resolutions in the Kubbealtı. Therefore, it occupies an important place in the history of the Ottoman Empire. For four hundred years, it was used for the same purpose. It was repaired and modified a few times and acquired its final design and decorations during the reigns of Selim III and Mahmut II.

The Adalet Kulesi (Tower of Justice) is adjacent to the Kubbealtı. Its second story was built in the 19th century. Inside the tower, there is a **window with a grate** which overlooks the Assembly Hall of the Kubbealtı. Until the reign of Kanuni Sultan Süleyman, the sultans presided over the Divan (Council of State). When a commoner intruded the meeting one day to express his compaints, it was decided against the sultans attending the meetings. From then on, the sultans watched the meetings from behind this window and the area came to be known as "the resting place of the sultans."

The sultan tapped on the grate and interrupted the meetings whenever he wanted information from the Grand Vizier, who then met the sultan in the Arz Odası (Audience Hall). It is said that the members of the council were particularly careful not to make wrong decisions, since they never knew when the sultan might be listening. The Divan discussed the affairs of the state and the problems pertaining to the public. After the meetings, viziers used to eat together. The **Divit Odası** (writing room), the section where documents were kept, the rest areas and the tea rooms were all in the vicinity of the Kubbealtı.

AKAĞALAR KAPISI (THE GATE OF THE WHITE EUNUCHS)

The third courtyard in entered through the Akağalar Kapısı, which is also known as the Bâbü's-sa'âde (Gate of Felicity) and the Arz Kapısı, since it faces the Arz Odası. A verse from the Koran and the tughra of Mahmut II are inscribed on the gate, and on both sides of the entrance there are inscriptions in the shape of the tughra.

Many important events in the history of the palace and the Ottoman Empire took place in front of

The Kubbealtı, a scene depicting the reception of an ambassador.

this gate. The coronation of the sultans (cülus), paying homage to the sultans (biat), funerals, Ayak Divans, where complaints of the janissaries and the public were listened to, holiday greetings, and the presentation of the flag to the sultan leaving on a campaign traditionally took place here. Some of the miniatures and paintings depicting these scenes enable us today to get a better idea about these ceremonies. The "Protocol Notebook" explains in detail how these ceremonies were performed.

Undoubtedly, the most important ceremony was the coronation of a new sultan upon the death of the reigning sultan. The funeral, coronation and other ceremonies relating to these events took place on the same day, at the same place, i.e. in front of this gate.

Inside, on the left of the corridor with a fireplace was the quarters of the Akağalar (White Eunuchs) and on the right were the quarters of the Bâbü's-sa'âde (The Head White Eunuch), who was the most powerful chief of the palace, and the quarters of other high-ranking chiefs.

The Tower of Justice and the entrance to the Harem.

Selim III accepting holiday greetings in front of the Akağalar Gate.

ENDERUN, THE THIRD COURTYARD

By definition, Enderun means "inside." It was a place where the sultan spent a lot of time in the course of his daily life. The courtyard is surrounded by the **quarters of the Enderun Ağas (boys of the inside),** who were in the service of the sultan and palace. They were recruited from foreign lands (Devşirme) and brought to the palace after receiving a preliminary education in other schools. They both served the sultan and received an education. The palace was like an advanced school where one received an education and had a chance to apply what one had learned. Enderun Ağas were given a general education first, and then they were educated in various occupations and services. They also studied fine arts like music and script. General military education was not neglected either.

There were four classes of service: **Seferli, Kilerli, Hazineli,** and **Hasodalı.** The Seferlis (campaign pages) were in charge of the laundry of the sultan and studied fine arts. The Hazinelis protected the treasury; Kilerlis were in charge of the meals for the sultan, and the Hasodalıs protected the sacred relics. These were the Enderun Ağas closest to the sultan.

Today, the quarters of the Seferlis houses the Sultans' Costumes Section, the Fatih Pavilion and the former treasury house the Treasury Section, the quarters of the Kilerlis houses the offices of the Museum, and the quarters of the Hazinelis houses the Sultans' Portraits and other exhibits. The quarters of the Hasodalıs was located adjacent to the Sacred Relics Section, and it is used as an exhibition hall, today. Apparently, every effort has been made to remain faithful to the original functions of the buildings while arranging the museum.

ARZ ODASI (THE AUDIENCE HALL)

In front of the Akağalar Gate is the Arz Odası. It is surrounded by a wide eave supported by twenty-two columns. The fountain and the tiles on the facade and the marble balustrade give a certain distinction to the structure. Many important ceremonies took place here, too. Inside, there is a **throne with a**

The Akağalar Gate, 3 different views.

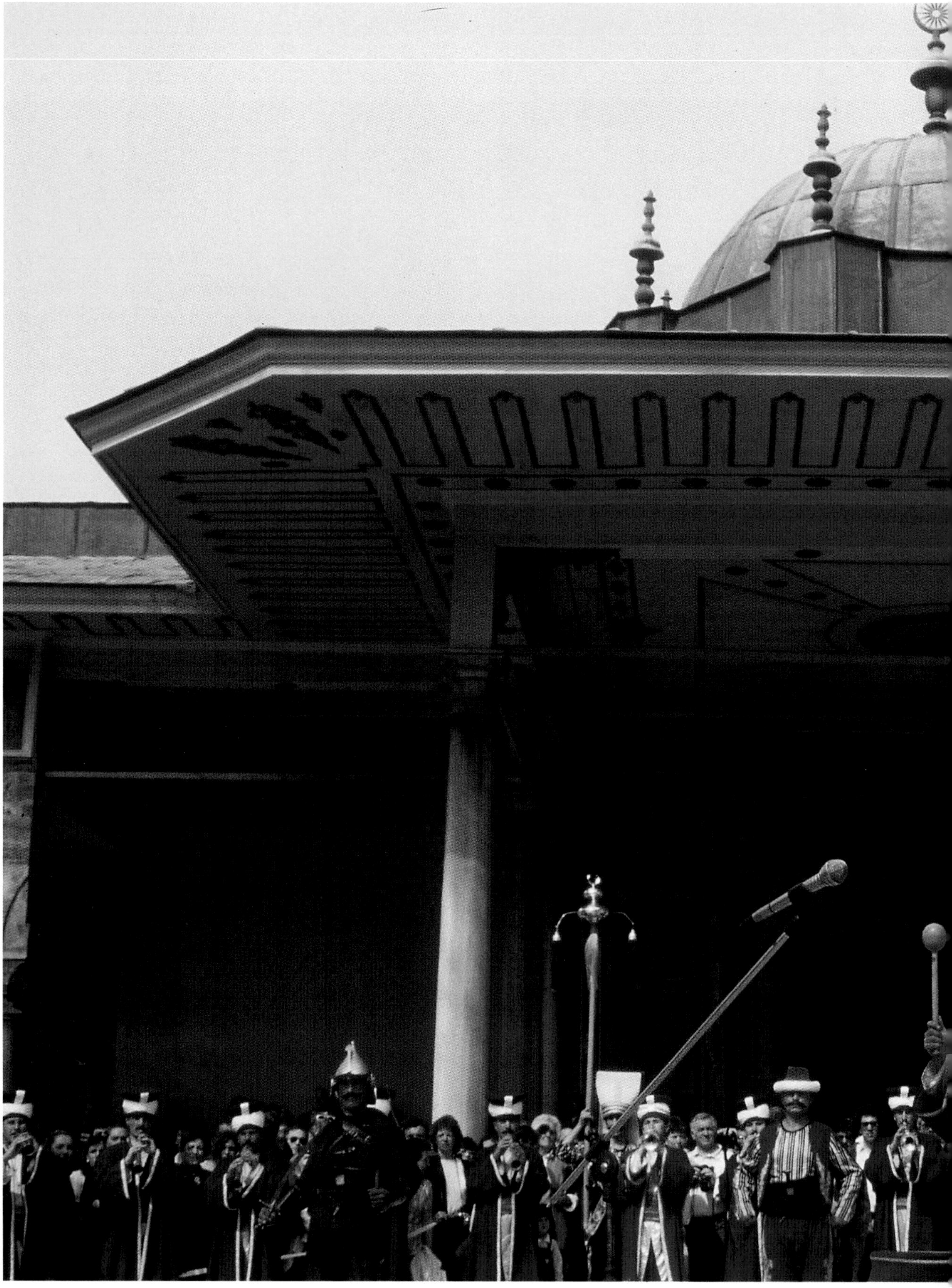

canopy where the sultans used to sit and accept foreign ambassadors and high-ranking officials, particularly the Grand Vizier. There are miniatures and engravings depicting these scenes. The ceremonies which took place here followed a certain protocol, too.

The tiles belong to the 15th century, and the canopy inside was made by Mehmet III. The inside of the dome of the canopy, supported by four spiral grooved columns, is covered by lacquered decorations of legendary animal and plant motifs.

The seat of the throne is covered by a jeweled cloth and there are pillows. The sultans' quilted turbans were kept in the built-in closet behind the throne. On the side facing the Library of Ahmet III, there are stairs leading to the courtyard from the portico.

The entrance to the Arz Odası.

The Arz Odası.

The Arz Odası.

A view of the Arz Odası.

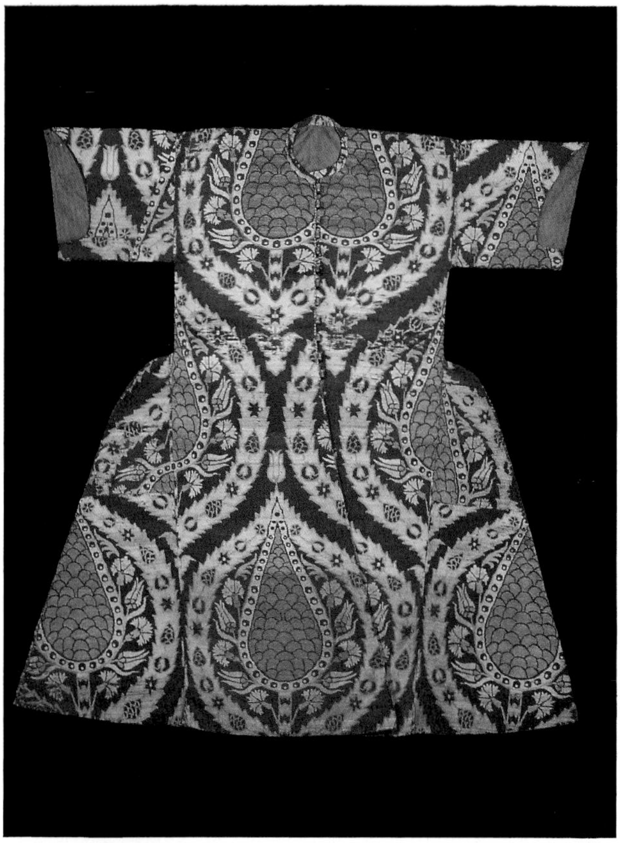

SULTANS' COSTUMES

Even though this section is called the Sultans Costumes, the caftans, which were the traditional outer garments of the sultans, and therefore of the Turks, are displayed.

Caftan is a garment which is open in front and tied at the waist by a belt or a sash. Above the waist, it is closed by buttons or cords. They were worn over under-garments. Some of the caftans on display are lined with fur. Some are made of famous Turkish fabrics like çatma, kemha, sof, etc. The caftan was a style of garment worn by the Turks in Central Asia before they had come to Anatolia. They used to be given as gifts to successful state and military leaders.

Şalvar (baggy trousers), which is another traditional Turkish garment, was worn under the caftan. Trousers were first worn during the reign of Mahmut II (1785-1839), as a result of relations with Europe.

According to an old Turkish tradition, which is still practiced today, when the head of a household

Three different sultan and crown prince caftans.

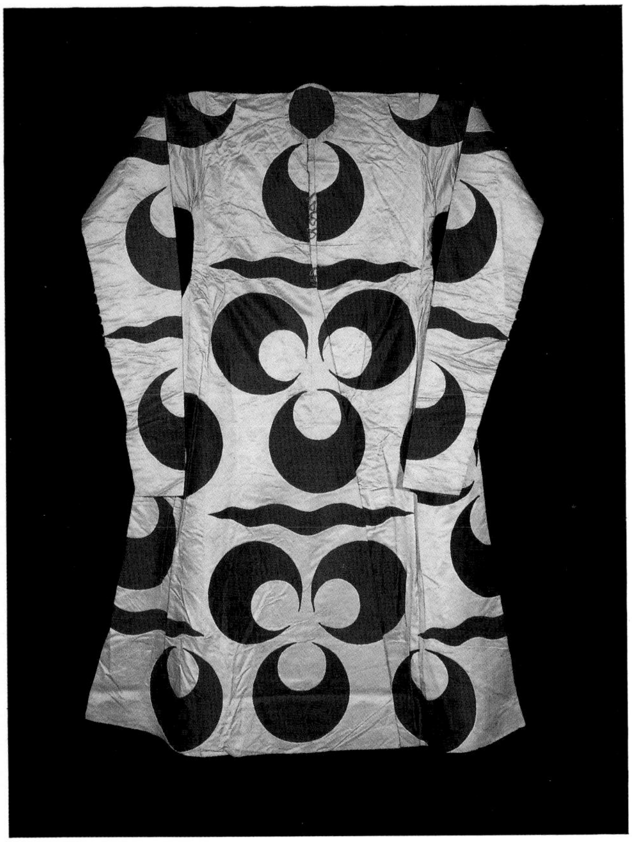

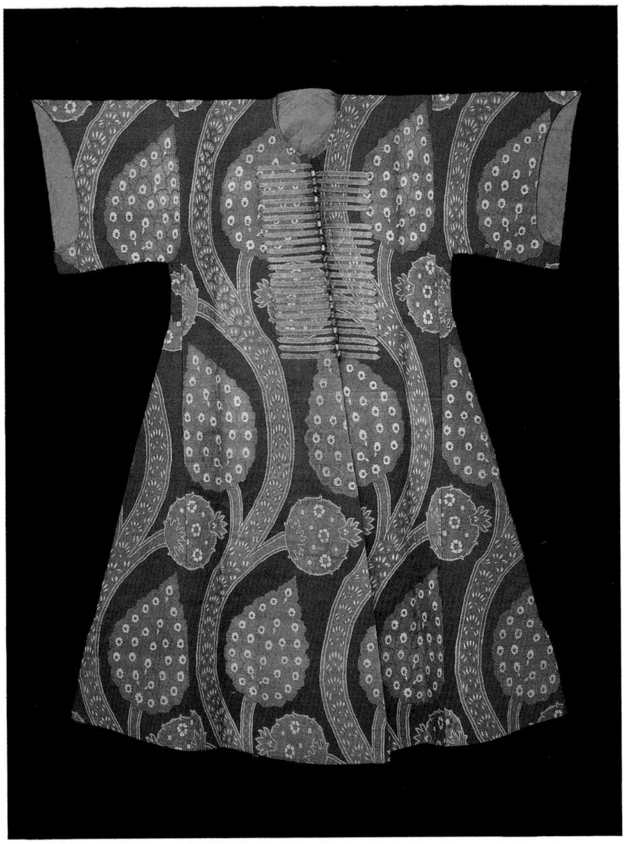

dies, his clothes are wrapped in a bundle and stored. This is why garments of the sultans are so well preserved. The garments of famous state leaders were wrapped and placed in the mauseoleums built for them. At the Topkapı Palace the garments of all the sultans succeeding Fatih Sultan Mehmet are displayed.

One not only views the garments in this section but also gets a change to learn about the **famous Turkish fabrics** they are made from. In the inner room connected to the large display hall, there are examples of these fabrics. Woven fabrics like sof, bürümcük and çuha were plain, but silk fabrics like canfes and atlas sometimes had designs.

Turkish fabrics like kemha, çatma (Bursa velvet) and seraser (gold threaded fabric) are well known for their designs which varied over the years. During the 14th and 15th centuries, large designs were used. Toward the end of the 15th century, the designs became smaller, but increased in variety. The Turkish art of weaving advanced remarkably during the 16th and 17th centuries.

In the 14th, 15th and 16th centuries **the motifs**

Sultans caftans and a shirt with a writing of a prayer.

Various Ottoman military uniforms.

used were of Central Asian origin. These were circles inside each other meeting at one point, speckles, Chinese clouds, etc. Later plant motifs like carnations, tulips, curved branches, branches with blossoms, leaves and fruit motifs like pomegranate and apple became predominant.

Unfortunately, the womens garments were not stored like the men's. The wives and the mothers of the sultans left the palace soon after the death of the sultans, and their daughters either left the palace or were married and moved from the palace.

A portrait of Selim II. wearing a caftan made of "Çatma".

Ahmet III and Crown Prince Mustafa

An exterior view of the Treasury Section.

A ceremonial helmet studded with jewels (17th century).

TREASURY SECTION

The pavilion built by Fatih Sultan Mehmet on the remnants of a Byzantine structure was probably the first residence of the Sultan. It later housed the treasury and this tradition continued even after the palace became a museum. In the basement of the building, a small structure resembling a chapel still exists. When it was built around 1475, the Harem had not been constructed yet. It is not known definitely, but the building was turned into the treasury probably by Sultan Selim. The palace treasury was very rich during his reign. As a matter of fact, for centuries the treasury was sealed by the seal of Yavuz Sultan Selim. It was opened and closed by members of the treasury ward with a ceremony.

There was a bath between the quarters of the Seferli, which houses the Sultans' Costumes Section today, and the Treasury building. The bath was built by Sultan Selim II. There is a rumor that he died there when he slipped and fell. There is an access from the first hall of the Treasury Section, which consists of four halls, to this bath.

Only the precious objects decorated with jewels and made of gold and silver are displayed in the Treasury Section. The rest of the objects which had been stored here for centuries have been moved to the appropriate sections after the palace became a museum (Porcelains, Costumes, Clocks, etc.). Also on display here are the precious objects which belong to the **Hırka-i Saadet** (the mantle of the Prophet) Section.

It is necessary to sort the objects found in the Treasury Section, the Sacred Relics Section and other sections of the museum into groups. In each section of the museum, similiar objects are displayed together, but in the Treasury, every object made of gold or silver and possessing jewels, except those made of fabric and leather, are displayed, Among these, household items, kitchen utensils, decorative objects and weapons are the most important. Until recently, even precious fabrics and jeweled harnesses were displayed here.

Until the 15th century, simplicity prevailed at the Ottoman Palace. Gold and silver objects were not used often due to religious beliefs, however, during the prosperous period of the Empire, a splendid lifestyle replaced this custom. The ambassadors and

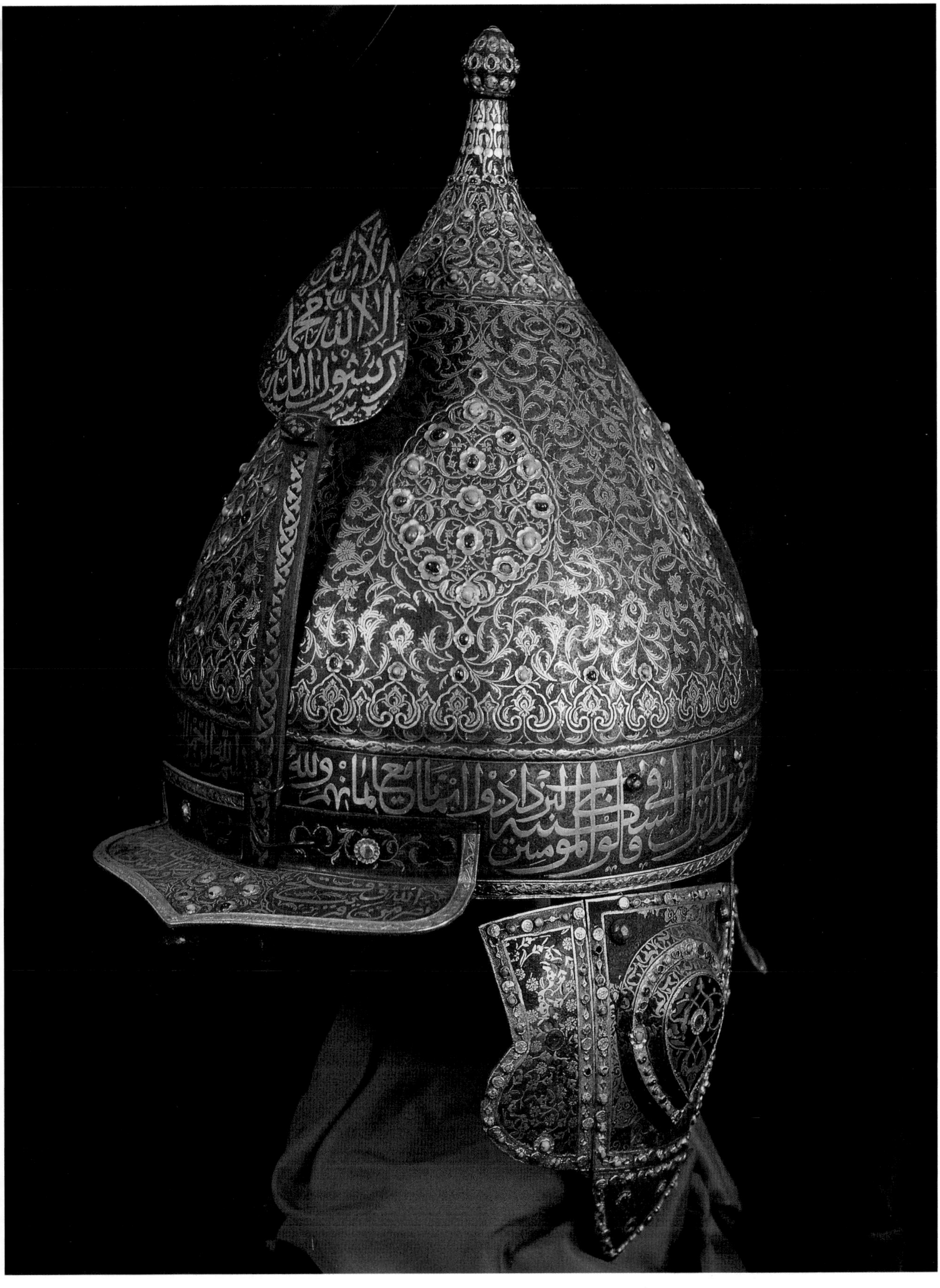

travelers who had seen the Topkapı Palace and attended banquets there talked about the grandeur. The jeweled gold and silver table settings were used and precious jewelry and garments were worn to exhibit the prosperity particularly when ambassadors visited.

The objects displayed in the Treasury Section are grouped as follows:

I. Those made in the workshops of the palace.

II. Gifts from foreign dignitaries.

III. Those brought from conquered lands.

IV. Those made in other cities of the Empire and presented to the sultans by Grand Viziers and viziers. Upon the death of the sultan, these were passed on to the palace.

The objects produced in the palace workshops were made according to the specifications of the sultans. It is not always possible to place them into particular group, or to group them according to the technique used in making them. Except for the manuscripts, miniatures and weapons made in the palace, very few objects were signed.

The objects displayed in the Treasury Section are made of metals like gold, silver, zinc, tombak (mercury plated copper) and a few are made of ivory, coral, wood or porcelain. They are embellished with diamonds, emeralds, rubies, pearls or enamel. The techniques used in the embellishments were reliefs, openwork, filigree, kalemkâr işi (pen work) and savat, (engraving in black on silver), and later applique was used. During the 16th century, there were more than one hundred jewelers among the group of craftsmen called the Expert Craftsmen.

In the Treasury, there are only a few pieces of jewelry belonging to the women. The tradition of passing the personal belongings of a woman to the treasury upon her death did not exist.

The objects displayed in the Treasury Section are neither grouped nor placed in chronological order. Yet certain similiar objects are displayed in the same hall.

In **the First Hall,** most of the objects exhibited are decorated with pearls and made of gold. Various **weapons,** including armor suits and daggers, embellished with precious stones, are on display also. These weapons were used during ceremonies. Zinc vases and bowls, objects made of gold, **model of a Chinese palace** and an **Indian music box in the shape of an elephant are worth seeing.** Most of

A glass pitcher studded with jewels (16th century).

Top: A ceremonial canteen (16th century).

these were presented to the sultans as gifts either from foreign countries or parts of the Empire.

Small objects are displayed in the right side of the showcase located in the center of the hall. Each one is a masterpiece worth examining closely.

In the long showcase located next to the wall, the gifts presented to **Abdülhamit II on the 25th anniversary of his reign** are displayed. The attractive **ebony cane,** decorated with rose-cut diamonds, was presented by Muslim Indians.

The **Second Hall** is reserved for objects embellished with emeralds. Uncut, half cut and even the most valuable emeralds used for different purposes are displayed. Peridot, although not as valuable as emerald, was used extensively in the Ottoman Palace. There is a large number of peridots in the showcase next to the entrance.

Emerald pins worn on the turbans of the sultans and emerald pendants hung in their rooms are exhibited in the showcase on the right. Undoubtedly, the most beautiful emeralds are found on the hilt of the famous **"Topkapı Dagger."** It was intended as a gift to Nadir Shah of Iran from Sultan Mahmud I. When the news of Nadir's assassination was heard on the way to Iran, the dagger was returned to the palace and placed in the treasury. At the tip of the hilt, there is a small watch with a lid. Previously, Nadir Shah had given an Indian-made throne to Sultan Mahmut I as a gift. The jeweled jade bowl sent by the Russian Czar Nicholas II is among the important objects displayed in the showcase.

The throne exhibited here belonged to Sultan Ahmet I. It is decorated with mother-of-pearl inlay and its canopy is embellished with rock crystal and other precious stones.

Rock criystal and jade were used extensively in the palace workshops. The objects **made of rock crystal** exhibit a unity in style. They have a definite shape, and they are decorated with plant motifs, gold plaques and precious stones. There are many examples of these in the long showcase along the wall to the right of the entrance. Before entering the Third Hall, a beautiful **cradle for the crown princes** is displayed in the showcase next to the door. It is encrusted with gold plates studded with precious stones. The pendant hanging on the wall of the same case is considered one of the most important pieces of jewelry decorated with rubies.

Top: A Ceremonial Canteen (16. century).

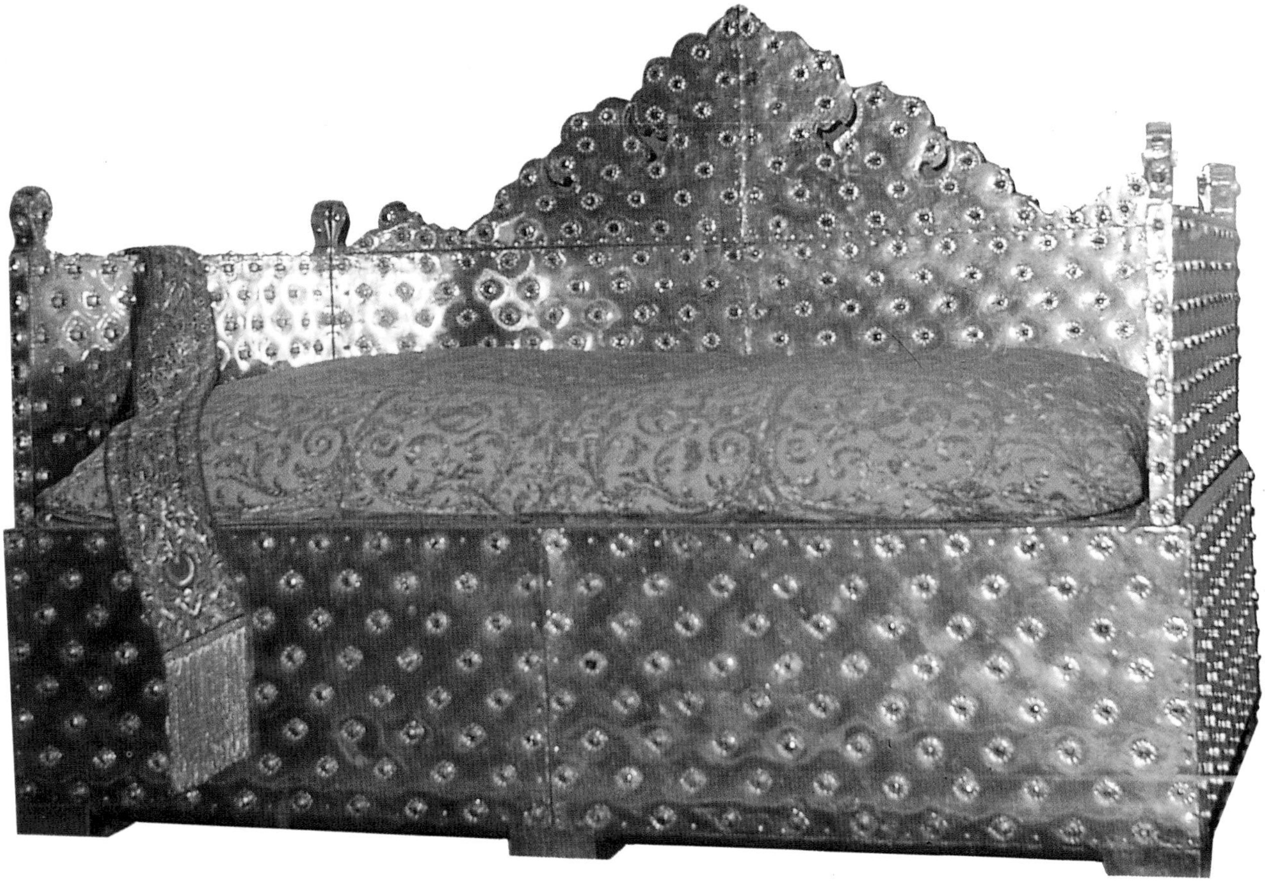

In **the Third Hall gifts, medals and diamond-studded objects from Europe** are displayed. Most of them are set with diamonds and some are enameled. There are many table settings and drinking sets. The medals were gifts from European, Persian and Russian monarchs. The eighty-six carat **Kaşıkçı (Spoonseller) Diamond** is the most famous and valuable piece in this hall. It is pear-shaped, faceted and surrounded by forty-nine large diamonds. Althought it has been accepted as the historical Pigot Diamond, sources indicate that it was traded for three spoons by a scrap seller, and therefore it is known as the Kaşıkçı Diamond. After the value of the diamond was recognized it was brought to the palace. In the middle showcase on the right, rings, broaches, earrings set with precious stones, and three famous and historical diamond pieces are displayed. These are:

- Kevkeb-i Durri
- Şeb Çirağ
- Silahtar Mustafa Pasha Diamond

The Kevkeb-i Durri was ordered by Sultan Ahmet I to be placed in the tomb of the Prophet Mo-

Top: The Holiday Throne.

A jewelled glass bowl.

A jewelled glass bowl.

hammed. The **two solid gold candlesticks,** each weighing forty-nine kilos, were ordered by Sultan Abdülmecit for the Kaaba. Thousands of diamonds embellish the candlesticks and the tughra of the Sultan is engraved on each candlestick.

The 16th century ceremonial **Holiday Throne** is displayed in this hall. It is covered with old plates and studded with peridots. During the holidays, the sultan sat on this throne, which was placed in front of the Akağalar Kapısı, and received holiday greetings. The throne is depicted in some of the miniatures.

In the center of **the Fourth Hall,** a very elegant **Indian style throne** is displayed in a glass case. It is covered with gold plates decorated with plant motifs and studded with thousands of precious stones. The throne was made in the 18th century and presented to Sultan Mahmut I as a gift from Nadir Shah of Iran.

The belt, armlet and cups displayed in the showcase along the wall on the sea side belonged to **İsmail Shah of Iran.** They were brought to the pal-

Top: The Nadir Shah Throne.

The Topkapı Dagger.

A jewelled ceremonial helmet.

ace by Yavuz Sultan Selim after the war of Çaldıran.

In the rest of the showcases, different kinds of objects are displayed. The first showcase in the wall to the right of the entrance contains gold and rock crystal **chess sets** studded with jewels, **snuff and perfume boxes,** etc. **Chinese porcelains** embellished with precious stones in the palace workshops are displayed in the rest of the showcase. **A gold bookcase studded with jewels,** a beautiful **collections of spoons** made of various precious metals, **the sword of Khalif Osman,** the curved knife of Kanuni Sultan Süleyman, and **rifles** decorated with precious stones and ivory inlay are displayed in the showcases along the wall on the sea side. Rock crystal and metal maces embellished with jewels were used by the sultans and men of the royal family during ceremonies. They were gifts from the artisans.

Among the different kinds of **boxes** on display, the one made in the 15th century by Uluğ Bey is made from sandal wood and it is a masterpiece.

The Spoonseller's Diamond.

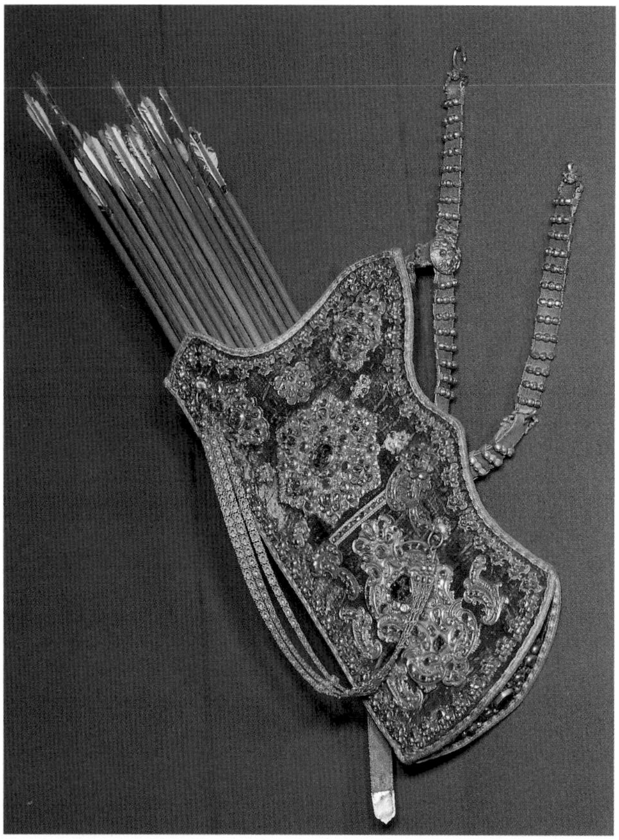

Quivers made of cloth embellished with embroidery and jewels.

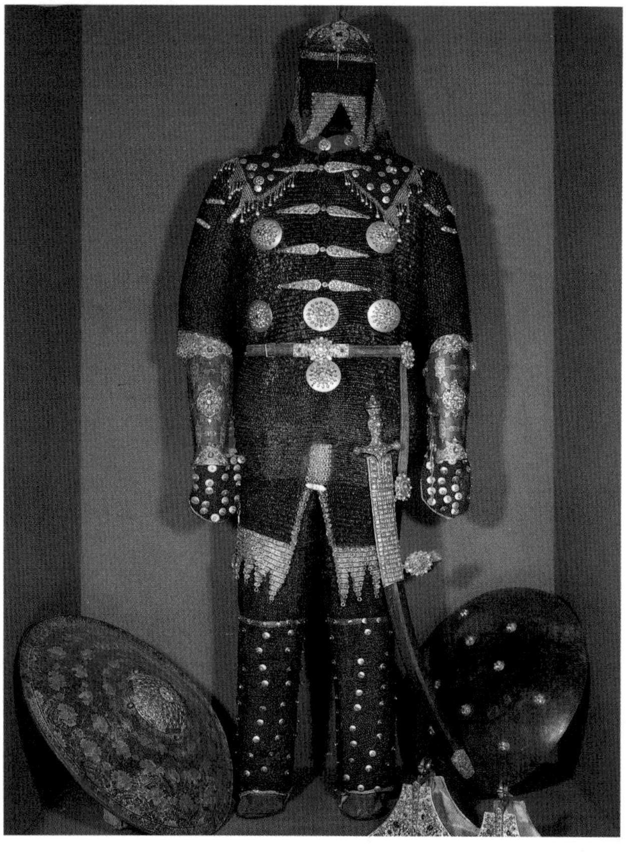

Murat IV's armor and sword.

The **relics** seen in the showcase to the left of the exit belonged to John the Baptist. **His hand, arm and skull bones** are encased in jeweled metal cases. No documents have been found explaining how and when these relics were acquired by the palace. Yet, we know that they were used as a bargaining tool by Beyazıt II to save his brother Cem, Fatih Sultan Mehmet's son, from the Knights of Rhodes and the Papacy.

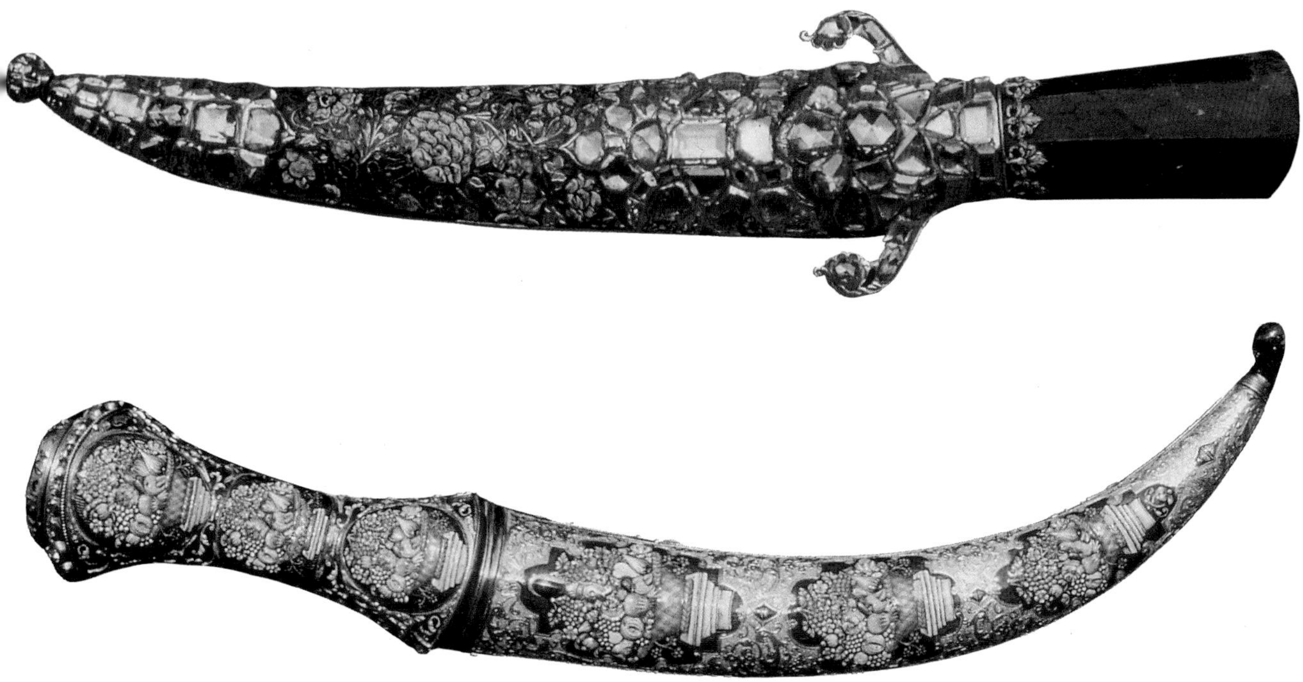

Top: Enameled and diamond-studded daggers.

A jewelled aigrette.

Top: A turban with an aigrette.

Bottom: A jewelled glass canteen and a rosewater dispenser.

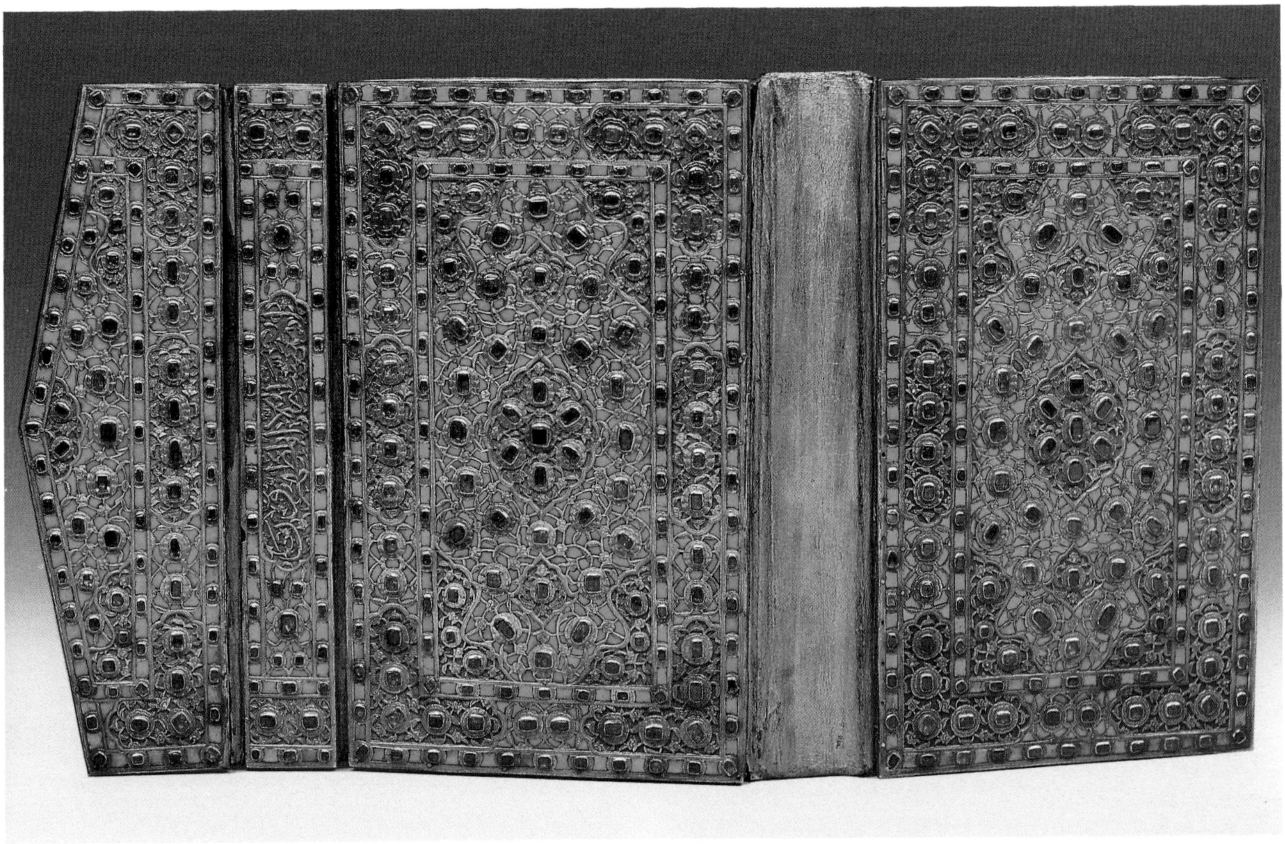

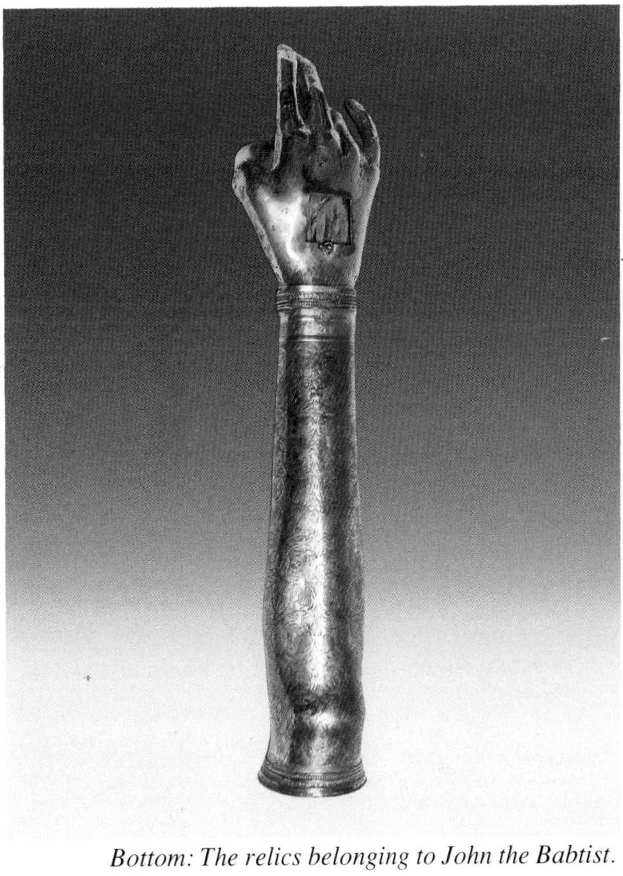

Top: An enameled, gold Koran case.

Bottom: The relics belonging to John the Babtist.

SULTANS' PORTRAITS

Portraits of the sultans are displayed in the second story of the building used formerly as the Treasury in Enderun.

The exhibit consists of thirty-seven pieces. Portraits of all the sultans are displayed in chronological order. Other portraits of the sultans, portraits of their women and state leaders are not displayed. Some of the portraits were in the palace and others were purchased from other palaces.

Artists of only a few of the portraits are known, and many of the portraits are copies of the originals. Portraits of Fatih Sultan Mehmet, Orhan Gazi and Selim II were painted by Italian painters.

Fatih's portrait was painted in 1907 by the palace painter Zorano from an original painting by G. Bellini which is now in the National Gallery in London. Kanuni Sultan Süleyman's portrait is probably a copy of the 16th century original, also.

Many of the portraits on exhibit are signed by **Constantine of Kapıdağ.** Under the patronage of Selim III, he painted many portraits and pictures, in-

A portrait of Mehmet, the Conqueror.

A portrait of Beyazıd II.

A portrait of Yavuz Sultan Selim.

cluding the portraits of Süleyman II, Ahmet II, Mustafa II, Selim III and the scene of a holiday ceremony. The portrait of Abdülaziz was painted by the Polish painter Clobowski. Aivazovsky painted Sultan Murat V's portrait and the Austrian painter Krausz painted Sultan Reşat's portrait.

THE CLOCKS SECTION

The clocks are exhibited in the former Treasury of Silahtar (Sword-bearer), located next to the Holy Mantle Section in Enderun courtyard. Although there are about there hundred and fifty clocks in the palace, only half of these are on exhibit and most of them belong to the 18th and 19th centuries.

About thirty of these clocks are Turkish. The rest were either purchased from Europe or presented to the palace as gifts. Watch-making in Istanbul started in the 16th century and the Galata district of Istanbul was the watchmaking center.

The oldest **Turkish-made clocks** belong to the 17th century and there are four of them. Later, the watch-making came under the influence of English

A portrait of Mahmut I.

A portrait of Ahmet III.

A portrait of Murat IV.

An Edirne-made Ottoman table clock (18th century).

A French-made table clock (Braquet 19th century).

style and in the 19th century other changes took place.

Most of the Turkish-made clocks are signed, and therefore, the names of the craftsmen are known. Since they embellished both the cases and the dial plates, the clocks are rare example of Turkish jewelry, wood and metal crafts. Majority of the watchmakers in the 19th century were Mevlevis, therefore some of the clocks made then are shaped like a Mevlevi headgear, which is a conical cap. The sultan was the patron of the watchmakers.

Most of the clocks are foreign made. In the collection there are many **English,** but also **German, Austrian, French, Swiss** and **Russian** clocks. These were brought by the ambassadors of European heads of state. Since the English clocks were quite popular, many **Markwick-Markham-**brand clocks were imported. Also, in the 18th century, many clocks signed **Le Roy** were purchased from France.

As the English and French clocks were made especially for Turkey, the numbers were written in Arabic and some of the clocks were decorated with scenes of Istanbul. Most of them play music.

HIRKA-I SAADET (THE HOLY MANTLE AND SACRED RELICS SECTION)

Personal belongings of the Prophet and objects from the Kaaba received proper care after they were brought to the palace. The Ottoman sultans realized the importance of the sacred relics and considered it a duty to the Islamic world to preserve and protect them. In the workshops of the palace, special jeweled gold or silver cases were made for these relics, and the swords were embellished with gold and precious stones. The chests and boxes made to store the sacred relics are among the most important objects at the Topkapı Museum today. A special staff of experts used to take care of the sacred relics, and the room in which they were stored had a special status.

After Yavuz Sultan Selim conquered Egypt, Ebul Berakat, the governor of Mecca, sent him the keys to the sacred cities of Mecca and Medina by his son Ebu Nümeyya, while Sultan Selim was still in Egypt. Historical sources indicate that most of the personal belongings of the Prophet and his disciples which are now kept in the Sacred Relics Section

A pocket watch with Abdülmecit's portrait.

A pocket watch with Abdülaziz's portrait.

were brought personally by Caliph El Mütevekkillillah III when he came to Istanbul to transfer the Caliphate to Yavuz Sultan Selim upon his return from Egypt. Some of the relics were brought later. The two most important relics are the letter of the Prophet (Name-i-Saadet), which was brought during the reign of Abdülmecit, and one of the swords of the Prophet, brought during the reign of Sultan Reşat.

The Sacred Relics are grouped as:

1. Personal belongings of the Prophet.
2. Swords of the Caliphs, disciples of the Prophet and other religious leaders.
3. Personal belongings of the caliphs, disciples of the Prophet, religious leaders and other prophets.
4. Korans, religious books and framed inscriptions.

Personal Belongings of the Prophet Mohammed

The Mantle of the Prophet (Hırka-i Saadet)

Undoubtedly, the most important sacred relic is the mantle of the Prophet. It is kept in a gold box which is wrapped in a precious cloth, and stored in a gold chest ordered by Sultan Abdülaziz. The mantle is made of black wool material and lined with a beige-colored fabric. The sacred mantle was acquired first by the Omayyads, then the Abbasids, and finally brought to the palace by Yavuz Sultan Selim. A special ceremony was held on the 15th day of each Ramadan, when the sultans paid a visit to the sacred mantle.

The Swords of the Prophet (Seyf-i Nebevi)

According to historians, the Prophet had nine swords. He gave the one called Zülfikâr to Caliph Ali. Another sword was left to the Prophet by his father. Only two of his swords are at the Topkapı Palace. They are decorated with gold and one of them is studded with jewels. They are displayed along with the mantle in the Throne Room. Another weapon belonging to the Prophet, a bow, is also on display. It is made of a material similiar to bamboo and has a **gilded case.**

The Letter of the Prophet (Name-i Saadet)

It is the letter written by the Prophet to Mukavkas, the Coptic ruler, inviting him to join Islam. It was found in 1850 in Egypt, stuck on the cover of an old book. Written on leather, it consists of twelve lines, and ends with the seal of the Prophet. There

An exterior view of the Sacred Relics Section.

An interior view of the Sacred Relics Section.

The keys to the Kaaba.

are six more letters of the Prophet on display, but these are in bad shape and are unreadable.

The Seal of the Prophet (Mühr-ü Saadet)

According to historians, the seal of the Prophet was passed first to Caliph Abubakr, then to Omar and then to Osman, who dropped it in a well. The seal displayed in the Holy Mantle Section was discovered in the middle of the 19th century in Baghdad and brought to the Topkapı Palace.

The Tooth of the Prophet (Dendan-ı Saadet)

It is a piece of his tooth, broken during the war of Uhut. It is kept in a gold decorated case ordered by Sultan Mehmet IV.

The Beard of the Prophet (Lihye-i Saadet)

There are close to sixty hairs of his beard in the Holy Mantle Section. Twenty-four of these are kept in cases decorated with gold and precious stones, or in boxes embellished with mother-of-pearl inlay.

The Footprints of the Prophet (Nakş-ı Kadem-i Şerif)

There are six footprints of the Prophet in the Ho-

The gutters of the Kaaba.

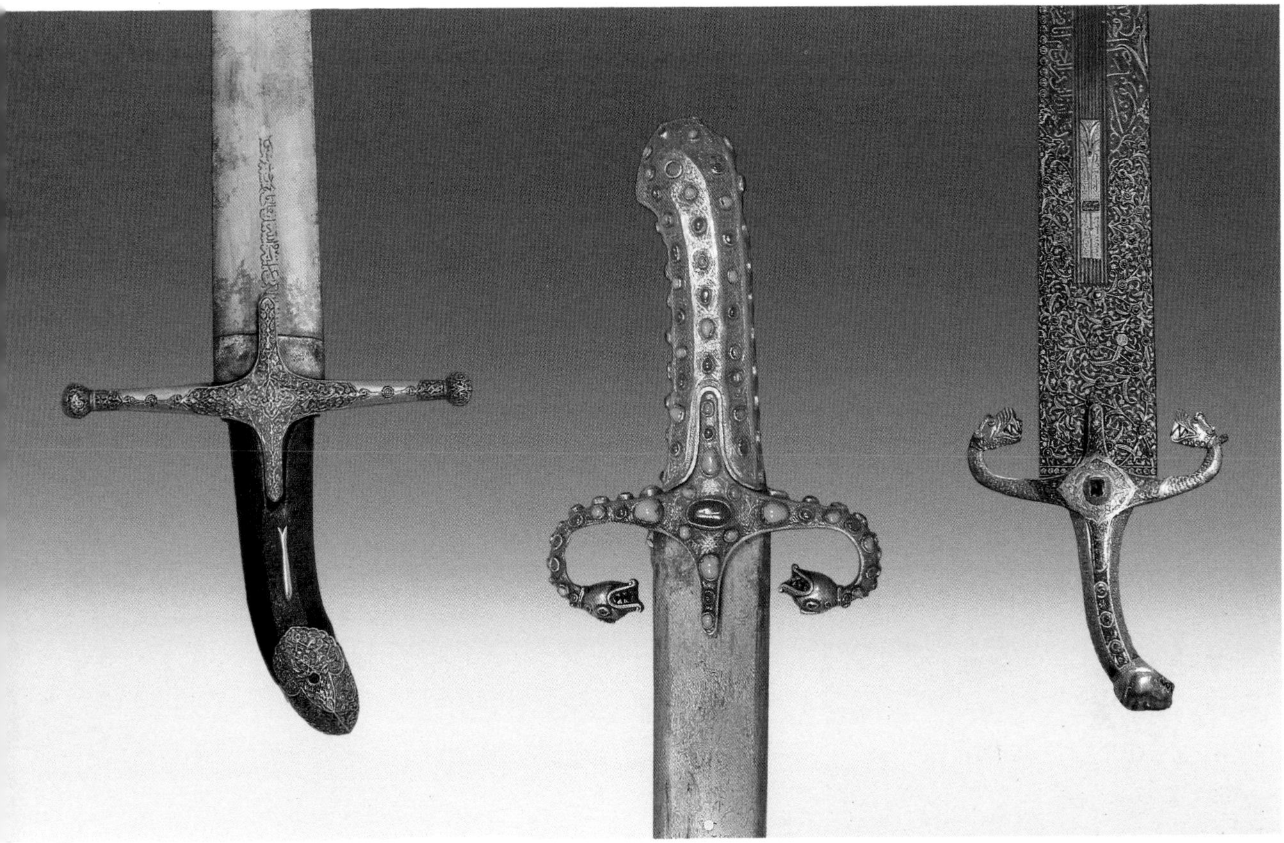

The swords of the Prophet and Caliph Osman.

ly Mantle Section. Some of them are in stone, some in brick. The stone with his footprint is supposed to be the stone he stepped on when he ascended into Heaven. It is displayed in a gold frame with a cover.

The Banner of the Prophet (Sancak-ı Şerif)

Sources indicate that the Prophet used one black and a few white banners, especially during wars. The black banner called Ukap, which supposedly was sent by Hayırbay from Egypt, is kept in a small chest. It was ruined by weather and extensive use. Later, pieces of the banner were sewn over a new banner made of green silk.

Other Sacred Swords (Süyufu Mübâreke)

There are twenty other swords besides the two of the Prophet. Except for the two swords which are assumed to have belonged to the disciples of the Prophet, owners of the other swords are known. Some of the swords were decorated with gold, silver and precious stones after they were brought to the Palace.

The swords and the religious leaders who owned

The footprints of the Prophet.

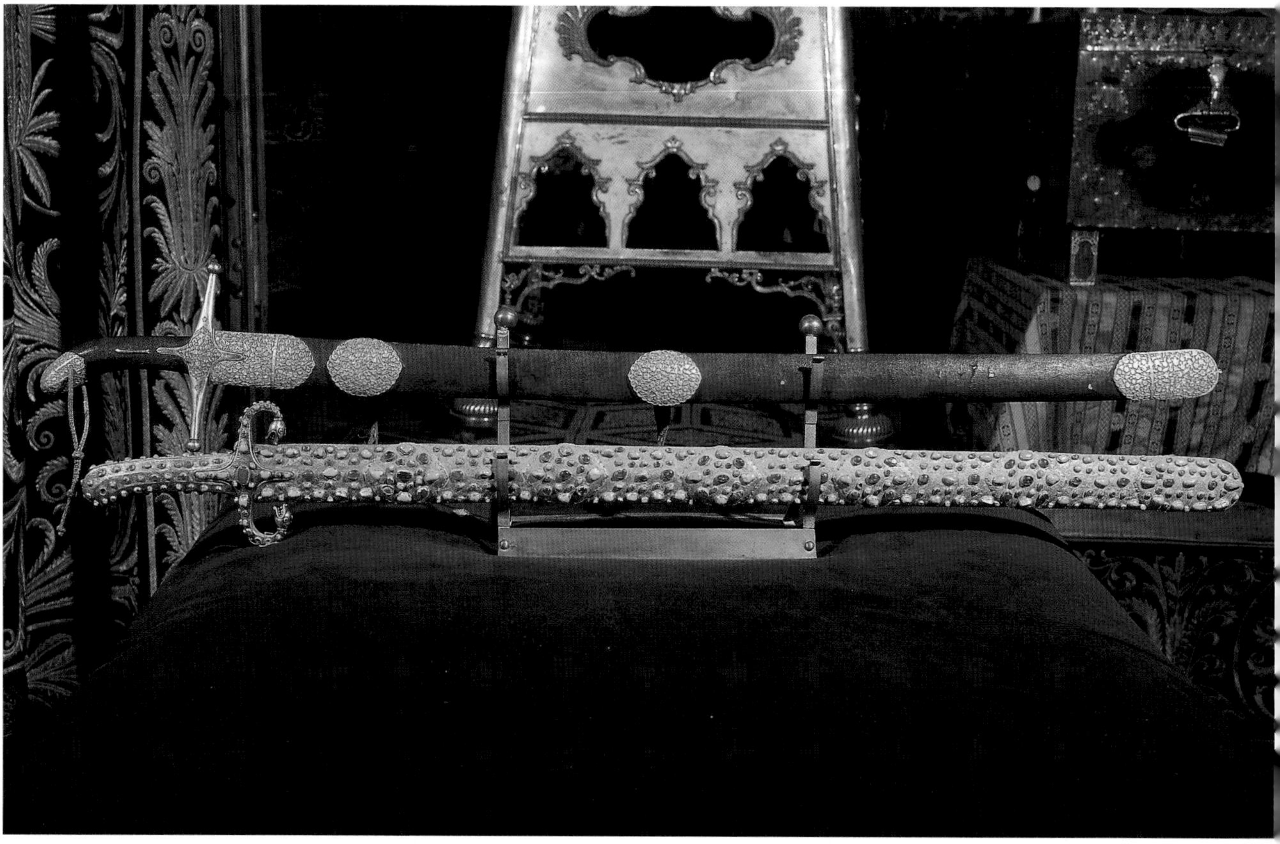

The swords of the Prophet in the Privy Room.

them are listed in chronolical order as:
- The Sword of Prophet David
- The Sword of Caliph Abukar
- The Sword of Caliph Omar
- The Sword of Caliph Osman
- The Sword of Caliph Ali
- The Sword of Companion Zeynel Abidin
- The Sword of CompanionAubeer Ibn-i al Avam
- The Sword of Ebul Hasan, secretary of the Prophet
- The Sword of Cafer-i Tayyar
- The Sword of Halid bin Velid
- The Sword of Ammar bin Yasir

Besides these, in the Holy Mantle Section, there are objects belonging to the companions of the Prophet and other religious leaders, many **Korans,** among which those attributed to the caliphs Osman and Ali, and **objects from the Kaaba**, Old materials left over from the restorations in the Kaaba are displayed also. Most important of these are the **cases of the sacred Black Stone (Hacer-i Esved)** in the Kaaba, **roof gutters, covers** and thirty-four **locks and keys** which have great artistic value.

THE LIBRARY OF AHMET III.

It is located behind the Arz Odası and bears the name of the Sultan who had it built in 1719. It contained 3,515 written works in Turkish, Arabic and Persian. When the Palace was converted into a museum, together with the books in the Revan Pavilion, these were moved into the Ağalar Mosque, located next to the library. Today, only the book covers are displayed in the library.

Located in the center of the Enderun Garden, this elegant building has a basement which was planned undoubtedly to protect the books from humidity. The narrow portico in the front is reached by stairs and there is a beautiful fountain in front of the portico.

Numerous windows let enough light in for easy reading. Inside, the 16th century tiles on the walls and mother-of-pearl and ivory inlay on the doors of the bookcases are exquisite examples of Turkish crafts. The subjects of the books stored in the bookcases are written on the doors. A script written by Ahmet III, who was a famous calligrapher, hangs on the wall.

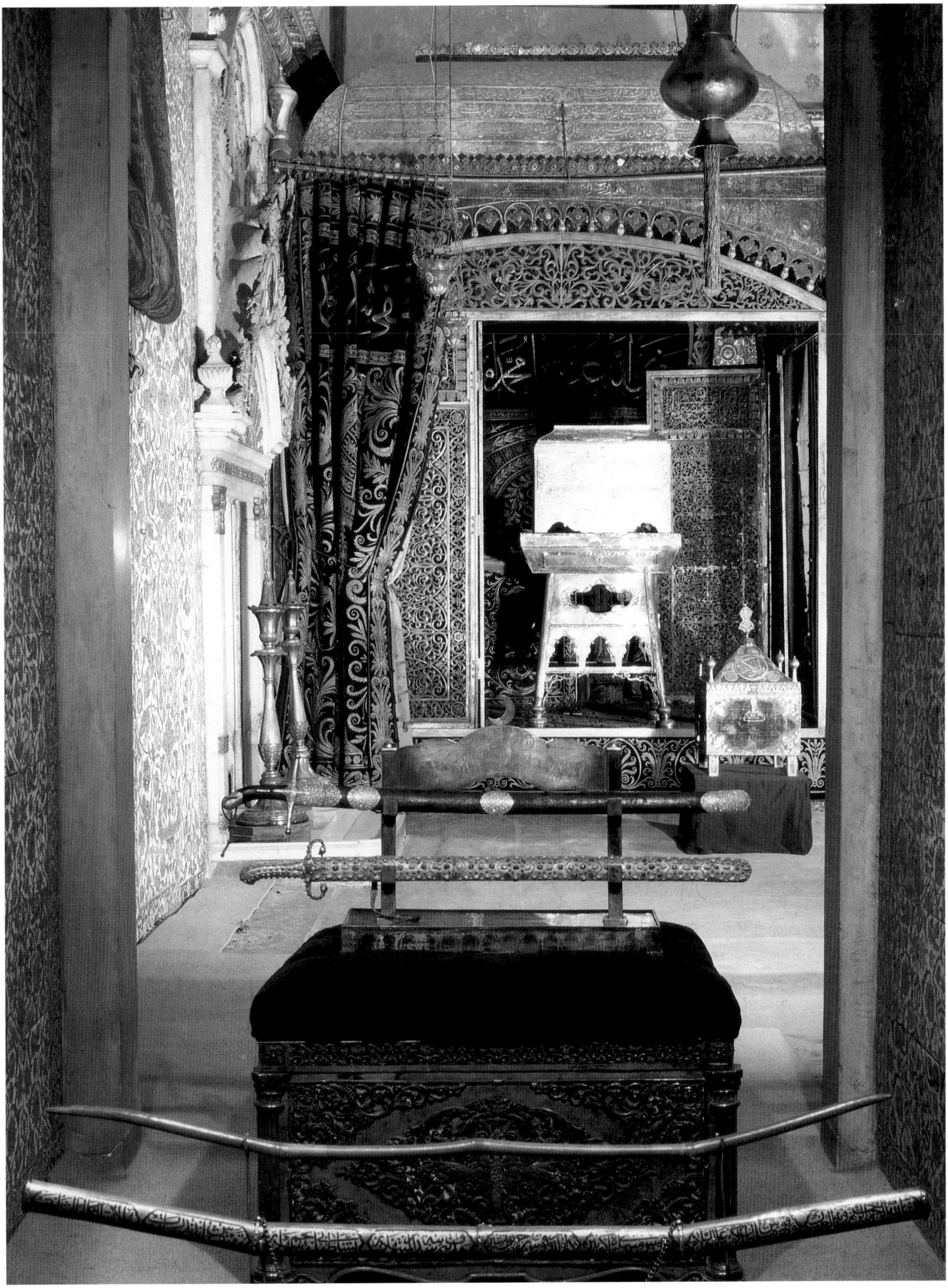

Two different views of the Library of Ahmet III.

A view of the 3rd courtyard.

Also, **the deed of trust** and **catalog of the library** and the **pickaxe used in the construction** of its foundation are exhibited in the library. The same pickaxe was used during the construction of the Sultan Ahmet Mosque, built by Sultan Ahmet I.

THE PAVILIONS

There are three passage ways, (one covered) from the third courtyard, Enderun, into the fourth courtyard. With its beautiful gardens and pavilions built in the corners, the fourth courtyard is more of a recreation area than a regular courtyard. As a matter of fact, the sultans and their families spent most of their time in these gardens and pavilions. Some of the famous merriments of the Tulip Period were staged here. Gardens built at different levels, pavilions expertly placed in corners, pools and fountains in the gardens are **characteristics of the "Fourth Place."**

On the north side of the fourth courtyard, there is a marble-paved terrace reached by steps. The big **pool with a fountain** in the middle is surrounded by the Revan, Baghdad, and the Sünnet Pavilions and a **baldachin.** The Pavilions are listed in chronological order as:

THE REVAN PAVILION: It was constructed in 1635 to commemorate Sultan Murat IV's Revan campaign. It has an octagonal floor plan and the interior is decorated with typical 17th century architectural embellishments. The stained glass windows, doors and built-in closet doors, decorated with mother-of-pearl and tortoise shell inlay, and tiles are worth examining closely. For a while, the pavilion was used as a library.

THE BAGHDAD PAVILION: It was constructed in 1639 by Sultan Murat IV to commemorate his Baghdad campaign. It is the most beautiful and elegant pavilion in the palace complex. It has an octagonal floor plan also, and the north side of the building rests on columns. There are wide eaves all around the building. The walls, both inside and outside, are covered with exquisite tiles of the period. The doors are decorated with mother-of-pearl inlay and the stained glass windows are beautiful examples of the creations of Turkish craftsmen. Below the stained glass upper windows, a tile frieze with

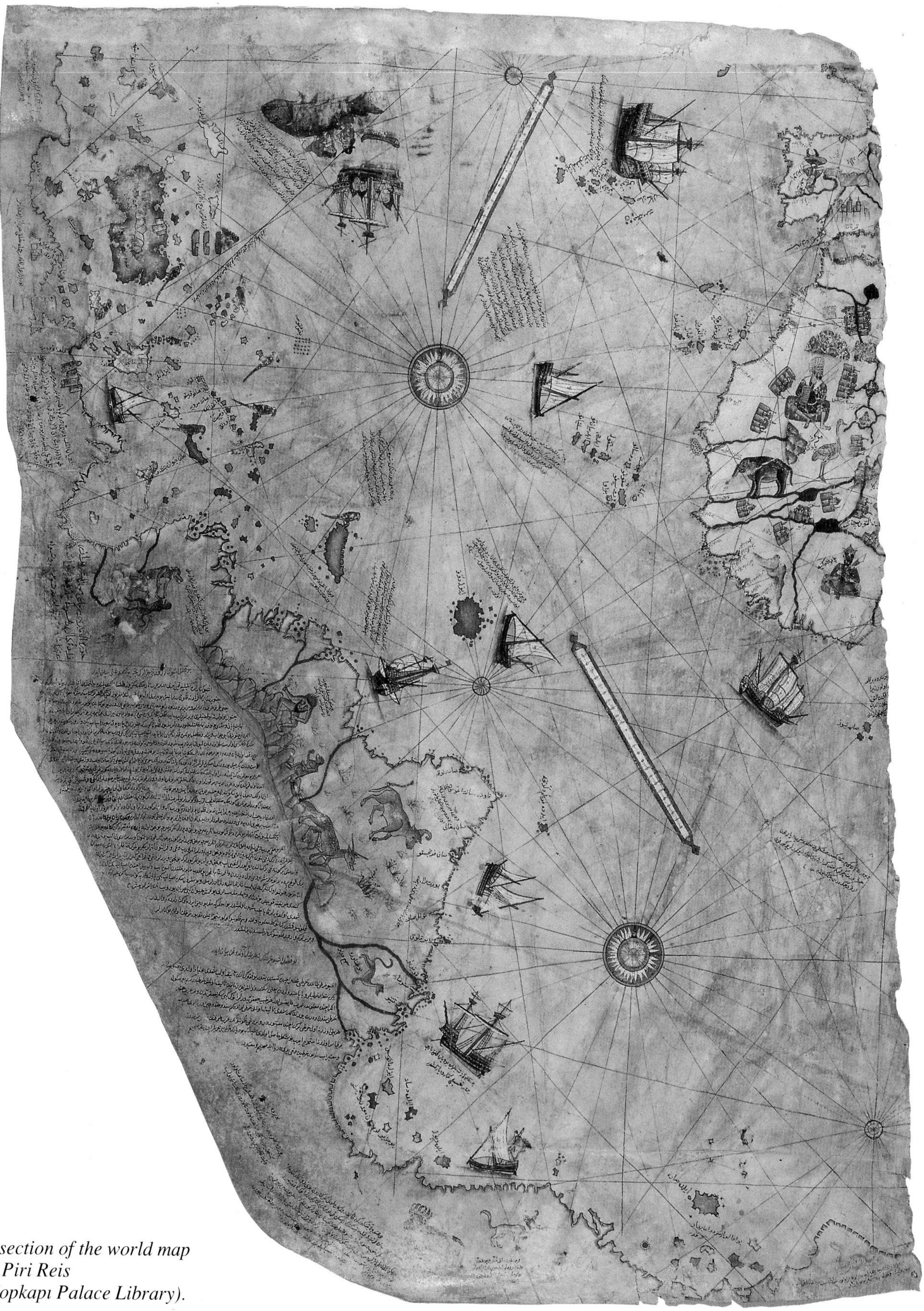

A section of the world map of Piri Reis (Topkapı Palace Library).

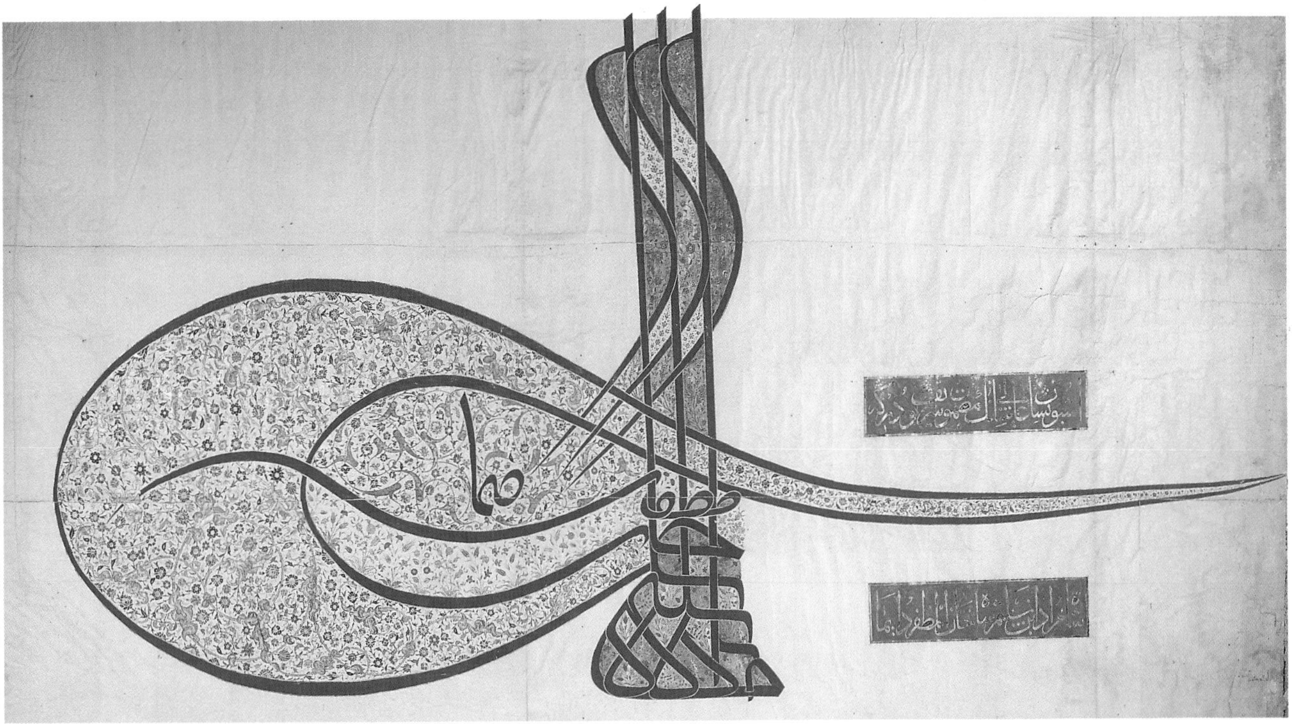

Tughra: The signature of the Ottoman emperors.

A page from the Mehmet Siyah's album.

Examples of Ottoman miniatures.

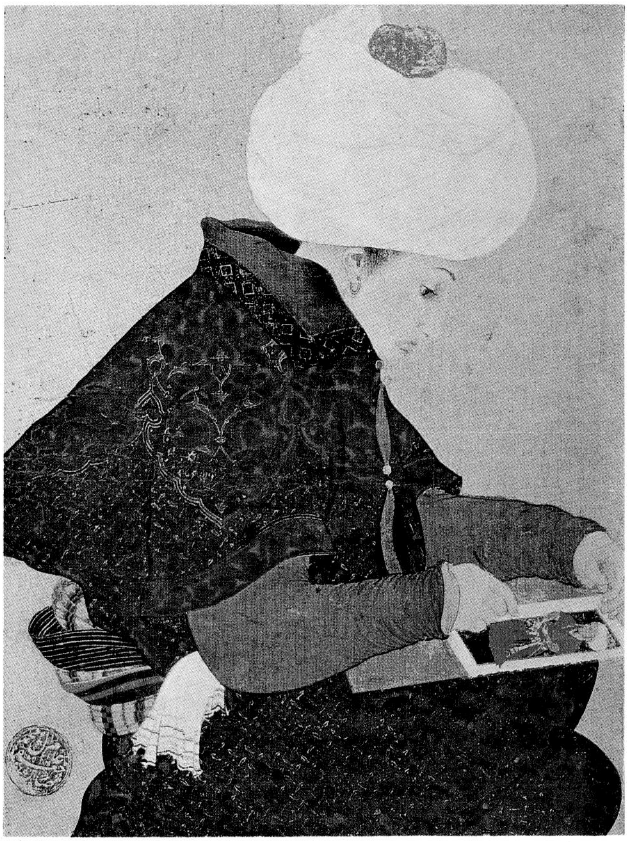

Top: Sultan Cem, Bottom: An Ottoman cavalry.

Top: The portrait of Mehmet, the Coqueror,
Bottom: An Ottoman lady.

inscriptions of verses from the Koran encircles the interior. The decorations on the inside of the dome and the geometric designs at its perimeter are rare examples of the Turkish art of embellishment. To the right of the entrance, there is a magnificent gilded-copper fireplace.

THE SÜNNET (CIRCUMCISION) PAVILION: Also known as the Circumcision Room, it was constructed by Sultan İbrahim I, who succeeded Sultan Murat IV, to imitate him. The walls on the south side are covered with exquisite tiles, both inside and outside. The tiles, particularly those on the outside, have interesting blue plant motifs with animal motifs dispersed among them. Inside, there are fountains in the window recesses and a gilded-copper fireplace. It is rumored that the royal princes were circumcised here.

The baldachin overlooking Haliç (The Golden Horn) was also built by Sultan İbrahim I. It is said that the sultans used to break their fast here during the month of Ramadan. There are verses and prayers from the Koran inscribed both on the interior and exterior of the canopy.

The Baghdad Pavilion.

The Baghdad Pavilion.

THE CHIEF PYHSICIAN'S ROOM

Originally, it was built during the reign of Fatih Sultan Mehmet as one of the towers of the wall surrounding the palace grounds. For a long time it was used by the chief physician of the sultans as a **pharmacy** and office. During the 19th century, it was used as a place **where the Enderun eunuchs practiced music.** For a while, it was used even as a **repair shop for weapons.**

During the reign of Mahmut II, there was a wooden story on top of this tower made of stone, but later it collapsed.

Behind the tower, there is a stone chair where Sultan Murat IV used to sit and watch the games played. Since the chief lalas (male servants in charge of the sultan's children) supervised the chief physician while he was preparing medicine, this structure is also called **Başlala** (chief Lala) Tower.

Today, only the two stories stand. After it was restored, everything related to medicine and phar-

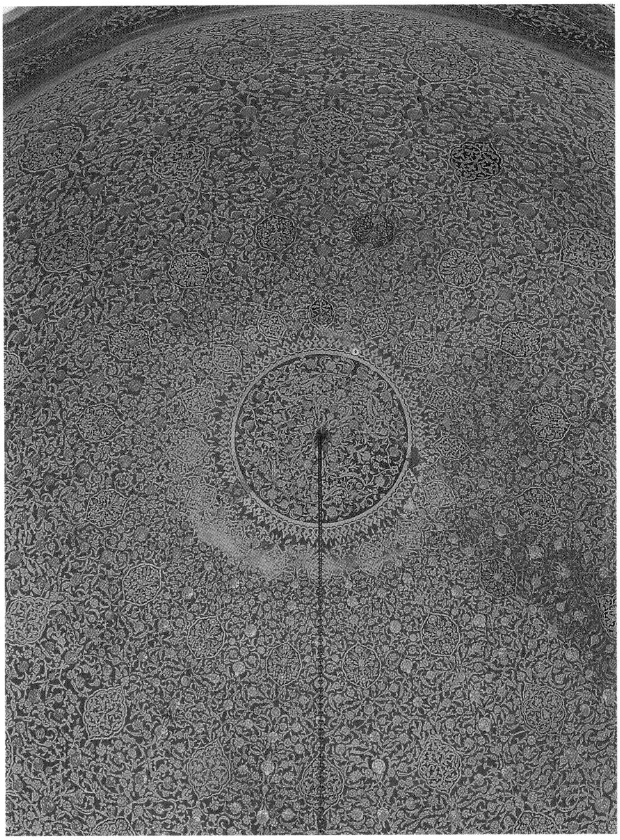

The gold-embellished interior of the dome of the Baghdad Pavilion.

A view of the Baghdad Pavilion.

The Revan Pavilion.

An interior view of the Baghdad Pavilion.

Top: The Harem as seen from the terrace. Bottom: The tiles of the Revan Pavilion and the Circumcision Room.

The Room of the Holy Mantle as seen from the outside.

Top: The Mustafa Paşa Pavilion. *Bottom: The Mecidiye Pavilion.*

The Quarters of the Karaağalar.

macy stored in the Treasury and other parts of the Palace were brought here, and in 1982, they were put on display. Drugs and pharmaceutical tools are exhibited in the first story. The second story is arranged as the office of the Chief Physician. Besides the tools he used, books and framed inscriptions pertaining to medicine are exhibited.

THE HAREM

Even though it was known as the Harem, the residence of the sultans and their women was also called **Dar'üs Saade** (the House of Felicity).

Not only in the Ottoman Palace, but also in the history of all eastern countries, due to the mystery surrounding it, the word Harem brings to mind the Harem of the Topkapı Palace. How much is know about the Harem which, in western literature, was a very popular subject, often embellished? In reality, due to the ethics of Islam and specific rules of the Harem, only the sultan, his family and a certain group of people in their service could enter the Harem. These restrictions intensified the mystery associated with it. As usual, because of natural curiosity toward anything prohibited, the Harem attracted exteme interest. A lot of fiction has been written about it, and imaginary and exaggerated life styles have been accepted as real.

Was it forbidden to describe the private lives of the sultans and their women? There are no documents on the subject and there is no need for it, either. The private lives of all the rulers in the world are kept secret. What made the Harem so different was the fact that nobody besides the principle employees of the Harem was allowed to enter. Harem means "a place forbidden to enter." Not even the grand viziers, viziers, ambassadors or other palace employees were allowed to enter. Only a few who did not belong to the Harem could enter it. These were the palace physicians, repairmen, piano and organ tuners, etc. What they described was just the building and furniture. Besides the physicians, nobody saw the women.

All the banquets and receptions for Turkish and foreign statesmen, meetings and audiences with the sultans took place outside the Harem.

Although life in the Harem is not known, information on its organization and the way it func-

Top: An exterior view of the Harem. *Bottom: The entrance to the Hünkar Sofası and the Hall with a hearth.*

The dome of the Murat III. Pavilion.

tioned is deduced from various documents. Food and wardrobe expenses indicate the number of people in the harem; documents on salaries and appointments give information on their titles, and the charities they were involved with give an idea on their character. Written documents such as orders, permits and accounts and even the letters sent by the sultans and high-ranking officials of the palace enable us to understand the organization and even the life in the Harem.

The Topkapı Palace was built by Fatih Sultan Mehmet, but the Harem moved here seventy years later from the Old Palace, located in the Beyazıt district of Istanbul. The date of the construction and the date of settlement into the Harem are disputed. Sources indicate that Kanuni Sultan Süleyman had the Harem built on the insistence of his wife Roxelane. The relocation of women into the Topkapı, Palace took place in stages and it was completed during **the reign of Sultan Murat III,** when the concubines, too, were finally moved in.

When the succeeding sultans built new buildings the Harem lost its original floor plan and became a disorganized complex. Every sultan did not live in the Harem. Some lived here periodically, some preferred the palace in Edirne and some lived in the private pavilions and palaces they had built by the shores of the Bosphorous or the Golden Horn.

Upon the completion of Dolmabahçe Palace in 1853, the Harem, in its entirety, was moved there.

The Harem of the Topkapı Palace consists of three main sections:

1. The Black Eunuch's section
2. The Women's section
3. The Sultan's section

For all these people there were about three hundred rooms, baths, lavatories, a hospital for the concubines and kitchens. The Harem, which occupies an area as large as a city district, consists of marble **paved courtyards surrounded by porches** and rooms. It is necessary to consider each courtyard and its surroundings as a unit.

From the palace, there are **two entrances** into the Harem: **The Arabalar (Carriage) Gate,** and the **Kuşhane (Saucepan) Gate,** through which the food was brought in. The traffic through both gates was controlled by the black eunuchs. All the buildings

between these two gates were reserved for the various services and the residences of **the black eunuchs.** The black eunuchs were sent to the palace by governors of Egypt and trained in the Harem under strict discipline. The Chief Black Eunuch was one of the people closest to the sultan, and he was one of the most influentiel people in the palace after the Grand Vizier.

The entrance located next to the Kubbealtı was originally the entrance to the Quarters of the Black Eunuchs. The women of the Harem used to leave through this gate and get on the carriages.

There are many rumors and legends about the first **room with a closet** located next to this gate. Further on the left is the Mescid (small mosque) of the Black Eunuchs. The walls of the Mescid and the walls facing open and covered courtyards are covered with tiles. On the doors leading into the courtyards, porticos and apartments there are inscriptions praising the sultans, and also the **deeds of trust.**

The gate of the **watch tower** of the palace, where the sultans listened to the discussions of the Divan,

The reading room of Ahmet III.

is located on the right of the courtyard. On the left are the the Quarters of the Black Eunuchs which consist of three floors. In the upper floors the Acemis (rookies) and the Ortancas (half-trained) lived. Kıdemli (experienced) black eunuchs lived on the first floor. Next on the left are the Quarters of the **Chief Black Eunuch,** and the **School for the Princes.**

The apartments of the women are grouped around three courtyards: the Courtyard of the Valide Sultan (Queen Mother), the Courtyard of the Cariyeler (concubines) and the Courtyard of the Gözde and İkballer (favorites). **The Courtyard of the Valide Sultan** is centrally located to control the rest of the Harem. There are passageways and doors leading into the apartments of the concubines, kadın efendis (wives of the sultan), princes', crown princes' and favorites from this courtyard located in front of the **Apartment of the Valide Sultan** which is the second largest one after the Apartment of the Sultan. It has a reception room, a bedroom, a resting room, a prayer room, a lavatory and a bath. In the back, it overlooks the Golden Horn. Sultan Selim III had an-

The entrance to the Fruit Room of Ahmet III.

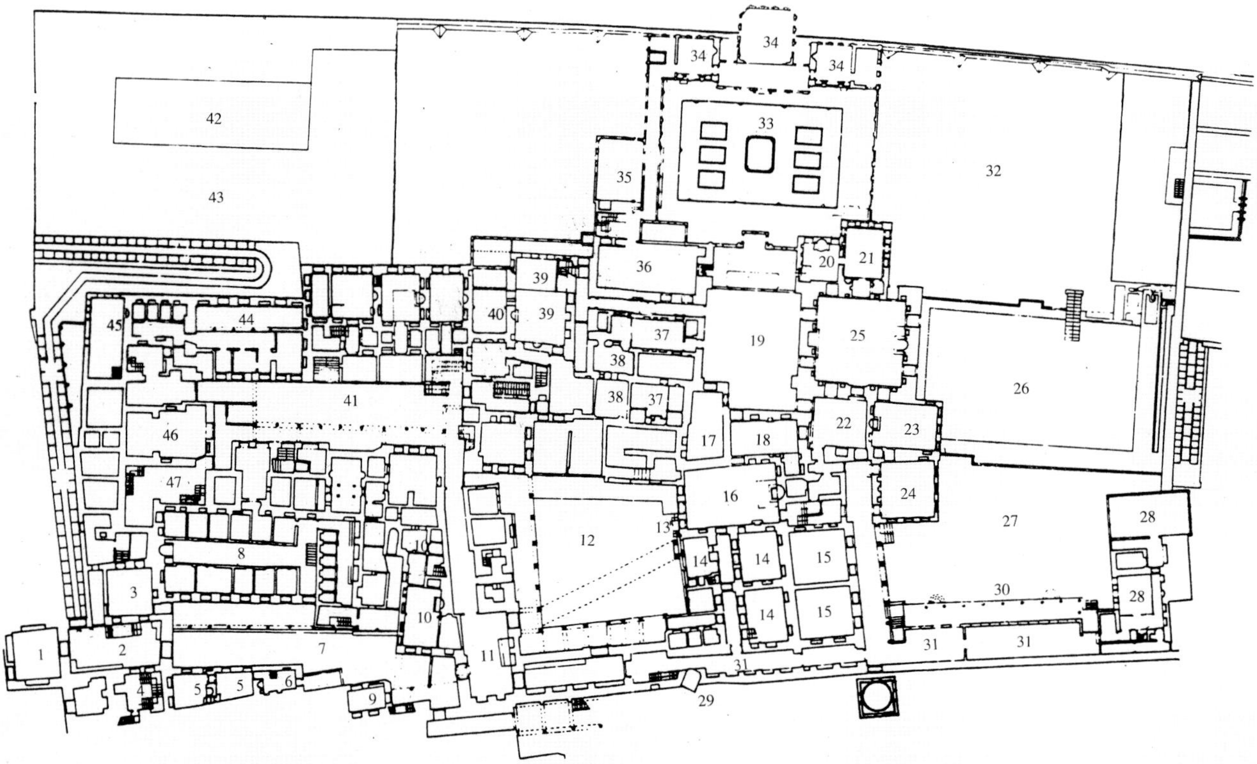

Plan of the Harem

1- The Carriage Gate.
2- The Hall with a Fountain and the Mounting Stone.
3- The Mosque of the Black Eunuchs.
4- The Tower of Justice.
5- The Apartment of the Bookkeepers.
6- The Quarters of the Palace Dwarfs.
7- The Terrace of the Black Eunuchs.
8- The Quarters of the Black Eunuchs.
9- The Quarters of the Harem Treasurer.
10- The Rooms of the Harem Chiefs.
11- The Quard Room.
12- The Terrace of the Valide Sultan.
13- The Sultan ate.
14- The Apartments of the Wives.
15- The Treasury.
16- The Room where the Sultan and his mother met.
17- The Bedroom of the Valide Sultan.
18- The Hall with a Fountain.
19- The Imperial Hall.
20- The Fruit Room.
21- The Ahmet I. Pavilion.
22- The Hall with a Hearth.
23,24- Twin Kiosks.
25- The Pavilion with a Pool.
26- The Large Pool.
27- The Courtyard of the Favorites.
28- The Mabeyn Apartment-the Abdülhamit Pavilion.
29- The Exit from the Harem.
30- The Apartments of the Concubines.
31- The golden Road.
32- The Harem Garden.
33- The Terrace over the Harem Garden.
34- The Osman III. Pavilion.
35- The Room of Selim III.
36- The Bedroom of Abdülhamit I.
37- The Imperial Bathroom.
38- The Bothroom of the Valide Sultan.
39- The Hall of the Valide Sultan.
40- The Bedroom of the Valide Sultan.
41- The Upper Terrace of the Concubines.
42- The Lower Terrace of the Concubines.
43- The Hospital.
44- The Quarters of the Concubines.
45- The Music Room.
46- The kitchen.
47- The pantry.

The Hünkar Sofası.

On pages 88-89, The Fruit Room.

other story added for his mother Mihrişah Sultan.

The influence of every age is seen in the Apartmen of the Valide Sultan as well as in the rest of the palace. The influences of the 18th and 19th centuries are seen in the decorations. The walls are usually covered with tiles, and the ornamentations of the ceilings, domes and certain walls are frescos of plant motifs and landscapes. Its spacious bath is located adjacent to the sultan's bath.

Experienced concubines and the Kalfas (assistants), Ustas (supervisors of servants) and Haznedars (assistant supervisors) who ran the Harem under the supervision of the Valide Sultan lived in the apartments located adjacent to the Apartment of the Valide Sultan.

These apartments face a separate, **smaller courtyard** and each has an entrance hall, reception rooms, bedrooms, storerooms, a fountain and a lavatory. There is a common bath facing the courtyard. **The rest of the concubines** lived together in the quarters located on the slope down to the Privy Gardens. These brick buildings are still standing. Their private **hospital** had a patients' ward, baths, lavatories, various utility rooms and a Gasilhane (where the dead were washed in preparation for burial). A **long corridor** connects the Courtyard of the Concubines to the area where the black eunuchs stood guard. The marble shelves found in the corridor were used to place food trays during meal service. **The Courtyard of the Concubines** is connected through separate doors to the Apartment and the Courtyard of the Valide Sultan.

The Apartments of the Kadın Efendis completely occupy the north side of the Courtyard of the Valide Sultan. Also, the upper stories of the buildings located on the east and west sides of the courtyard were reserved for the concubines and supervisors who served the Kadın Efendis.

The first of the two baths adjacent to the Apartment of the Valide Sultan belonged to the Valide Sultan and the other to the sultan. The baths possess the characteristics of a typical Turkish bath. Each has an undressing room, a dressing room, a caldarium and a sudatorium which has a bath basin, a sink and private rooms. The bronze grill was put here later for security reasons.

The largest room in the Harem, the **Hünkâr Sofası** (Imperial Hall), separates the Apartment of

Three views of the tiles in the Harem.

the Sultan from the Apartment of the Valide Sultan. It is entered from the Courtyard of the Valide Sultan through the Ocaklı Sofa (the Hall with the Hearth) and Çeşmeli Sofa (the Hall with the Fountain), also through the entrance hall of the Apartment of the Sultan and **Sultan Ahmet III**'s dining room, called the **Fruit Room**. A **throne** with a canopy for the sultan, divans for the Valide Sultan, Kadın Efendis and Favorites, and a few other pieces of furniture are found in the Imperial Hall. Most of the furniture were gifts from European rulers and do not belong here. The balcony over the area where the women sat was reserved for musicians. Apparently, the sultans and women were entertained together here. The floor was covered wall-to wall with rugs, and the curtains were made of precious fabrics. In the center of the room dancers danced to the music and dwarfs and clowns entertained the sultans and women.

The **tiles** and **decorations** on the walls and inside the dome belong to different periods. Instead of Turkish tiles, Delft tiles imported from Europe were used. Both the tiles and the 18th century Baroque and Rococco style decorations indicate that the Imperial Hall was renovated during the 18th century. The pendants exhibit typical 16th century **Turkish**

The fountain in the Murat III's Room.

embellishments. A verse from the Koran is inscribed on the blue and white tile band on the wall.

The pavilion and the courtyard seen through the windows were built during the reign of Sultan Osman III. To the west of this pavilion are the Room of Selim III and the Room of Abdülhamit I, but they are not open to the public.

The Apartment of the Sultan:

Even though today it consists of a dining room and a reading room, originally it was built as a single unit by Sultan Murat III, and it bears his name. It was in essence a pavilion. With its fountain, fireplace, canopies, tiles and ceiling decorations, it is a typical 16th century structure. Later, in the beginning of the 17th century, Sultan Ahmet I added a **reading room** and Sultan Ahmet III added a dining room. The mother-of-pearl and tortoise shell inlay on the doors of the book cases in the reading room, and the wall decorations of the dining room are of very high quality and beautiful examples of the Turkish art of embellishment. Due to the lacquered decorations of fruit motifs on the wood wall panels, the dining room built by Sultan Ahmet III is called the **Fruit Room.** It was supposedly built in 1705.

The location of the bedroom of the sultans has not been established. Sources indicate that a bed and a mosquito net were placed wherever the sultan wanted to spend the night.

In the 17th century, the apartment built by Sultan Murat III was rearranged and the **Apartment of the Crown Prince** was added on to the north of it. This section, which consists of two consecutive rooms, possesses many characteristics of Turkish architecture. The embellishments on the linen fabric stretched inside the dome, the tiles, the stained glass windows, and the built- in closet doors decorated with mother-of-pearl inlay are worth examining closely. In each room, there are fireplaces and very elegant, double fountains in window recesses. The side of the building facing the courtyard is covered with tiles and has wide, decorated eaves.

After leaving the Apartment of the Crown Prince, the courtyard seen on the left is surrounded by the **Apartments of the Favorites** and on the north is the **Mabeyn of Sultan Abdülhamit I** (private apartment of the Sultan where he received the viziers). Although all of these apartments were built in the 18th century, sources indicate that during the

Top: *The Courtyard of the Favorites and the Havuzlu Pavilion.*

The Courtyard of the Favorites and the Abdülhamit I. Pavilion.

Two examples of Ottoman attire (18th century).

reigns of previous sultans other importants buildings had existed here.

The Golden Way: It is a narrow passageway which stretches from one end of the Harem to the other and connects the Courtyard of the Black Eunuchs and the terrace of the Sacred Relics Section. Once, its walls were covered with tiles. It is claimed that during the holidays the sultans used to throw gold pieces to the concubines as they walked down the passageway. Therefore, it is called the Golden Way.

There is a stairway leading to the rooms of the Kadın Efendis, their concubines and assistants.

LIFE IN THE HAREM

The most important and powerful woman in the Harem was the Valide Sultan, mother of the Sultan. Then came, in order, the Kadın Efendis (wives of the sultan), favorites, odalisks, supervisors and concubines, who were the least important. The concubines were chosen from minority groups, or were given as gifts to the sultans by governors, state leaders, or sisters of the sultans. They were brought from different lands, but most of them were from the Caucasus. For centuries, Circassian concubines were favored because of their beauty, talent and elegance.

When they first came to the palace, **the concubines** were given a medical examination and then, according to their beauty and talent, they were separated into groups. Each one was educated differently. The beautiful ones were assigned to the services of the sultan and the rest were trained to serve in different services of the Harem. Experienced concubines, called Haznedars and Ustas (supervisors), were responsible for the education of the new concubines. Concubines were separated into three groups: Acemis (rookies), Ustas (supervisors) and Kalfas (assistants).

The number of concubines in the Harem varied in the reign of each sultan. In the beginning, there were few, but starting with Sultan Selim III, the number of concubines increased, and once there were as many as one thousand two hundred concubines in the Harem. All of them received satisfactory salaries and after a certain period of time, except for the odalisks, they could leave the palace. Some

Roxelane.

Hanım Sultan.

of them were married to high-ranking civil servants and their wedding expenses were paid by the palace. The Haznedars and Kalfas, after nine years of service in the Harem, could leave the palace or ask the sultan's permission to get married.

The sultans could spent the night with any of the concubines they wanted. Yet, in the history of the Ottoman Empire, there have been many concubines who refused to spend a night with the sultan, in spite of his strong desires. Documents indicate that Abdülhamit I and Abdülhamit II were turned down by a few concubines. This indicate that the sultans did not have indefinite authority. It can also be interpreted as respect for women.

Sultans sometimes were not content with the women of the Harem only, but developed relationships with other women in Istanbul, whose fame they had heard of. In order not to nurture jealousy among the women of the Harem, with the help of their sisters and the Grand Viziers, they kept these affairs secret. Sultan Mustafa III was involved in such an affair, and letters about the relationship have been found.

In the Ottoman Palace, there were also sultans who were not fond of women. Osman III was one of them. The rumor is that, since he did not want to see any women, he used to wear shoes with soles studded with nails, while walking in the Harem, so the women would hear him coming and hide.

There are many stories about how and when a concubine attracted a sultan's attention and became his **odalisk.** In reality, the sultans met their concubines sometimes by coincidence, sometimes after hearing them sing, or even by creating circumstances. The concubine they wanted was prepared by the special people in charge. The women who spent even one night with the sultan became a **Privy Odalisk** and was given a private apartment and concubines to serve her. If she bore a child from the sultan, she became a **Kadın Efendi.**

If a sultan's first Privy Odalisk had a son, then she became the First Woman, and therefore, she usually became a **Valide Sultan** later. If a sultan did not like his concubine, he could marry her to one of his employees and get her out of the palace.

The wives of the sultans were called **Kadın Efendis** and there could be as many as eight. They were called the First Woman, Second Woman, etc.

The ladies of the Harem during a walk in a parle (19th century).

The favorites and odalisks who bore the sultan a son could become a Kadın Efendi if the sultan so desired.

Once they became a Kadın Efendi, they were given their private apartments and concubines. When their sons were old enough to become govenors in the provinces, they left Istanbul with their sons and lived in the provinces for a long time. Later this tradition was changed, and they remained in the palace.

Upon the death of a sultan or his dethronement, his mother, wives, sisters and daughters were moved to the Old Palace. A Kadın Efendi could return to the palace only if her son became the sultan She then became the Valide Sultan.

Since the relationship between the sultans and their wives and odalisks was not always the same and sometimes the sultans were more interested in a new odalisk. Jealousy and the resulting intrigues were quite prevalent in the Harem. Most of these intrigues stemmed from the desire of each Kadın Efendi to have her son become the sultan.

If a sultan was weak or ineffectual, or a crown prince who ascended the throne was a child, then the Valide Sultan and his sisters became involved in the affairs of the state. Usually, the wives of the sultans were quite respectful to each other. When they wanted to go out into the city, they took their assistants and concubines along with them. One of the black eunuchs always sat next to the driver of the carriage.

In the beginning of the 19th century, during the reign of Mahmut II, the women of the Harem started the tradition of going out on excursions and this tradition continued.

When they went out of the palace, the women wore a Çarşaf (over garment) or a Ferace (a light coat). In the palace, they used to hide their long braided hair in a Hotoz (headgear for women), or wore aigrettes or tiaras. The loose dresses they wore were left open from the waist up and they wore belts with jeweled buckles. During the summer they wore silk dresses and in winter they wore dresses trimmed with fur. They also wore makeup and perfume.